2,000 ACCIDENTS

2,000 ACCIDENTS

A shop floor study of their causes
based on 42 months' continuous observation

Philip Powell (*Project Manager*)

Mary Hale

Jean Martin

Martin Simon

Project Designer: R. B. Buzzard

Statistical Adviser: J. F. Nuttall

NATIONAL INSTITUTE OF INDUSTRIAL PSYCHOLOGY

14 Welbeck Street, London W1M 8DR

1971

First published 1971 by
National Institute of Industrial Psychology.

SBN 901394 05 X

Printed and bound in England by Edward Mortimer Limited
Halifax and London.

Foreword

by the Right Hon the Earl of Halsbury FRS

Estimates of the cost of accidents at work in this country suggest that we lose something like £500 million in the course of a year. The cost in terms of pain, incapacity or bereavement is incalculable.

The research reported here is remarkable in that its data were collected by observers who stayed in four industrial workshops for a year and more. The authors therefore write with the confidence of close personal knowledge of what happens in the workshop.

Besides describing realistic ways of reducing accidents the report shows that neither unions nor management establish effective communication with the shop floor and this to a large extent sets conventional prevention schemes at nought. The report also provides insight into the way that lack of communication bedevils several other industrial problems.

I recommend this report to anyone who wishes to see the accident rate in industry reduced as part of the process of humanising our industrial system and increasing its productivity.

Acknowledgements

This project was undertaken with the joint support of the Ministry of Technology and the Ministry of Labour, now the Department of Trade and Industry and the Department of Employment. We gratefully acknowledge their support and encouragement, together with that of the managements, unions and the thousand people who co-operated with us over the four years' work. The authors also wish to record with thanks the names of their team-mates who did most of the work:

Paul Branton
Michael Creagh
Andrew Hale
Simon Jarman
Christine Lord
Joe Marsh

Tony Minchin
Mary Peett
Shelley Radice
Ron Stockbridge
Kay Thomas
Caroline Warne

and statistical assistants:

Maurice Bradley
Jayne Davies
Julian Fuller
Phillip Hollis

Nasir Khan
Christine Marinowitz
Ruth Sage
Frank Saunders

and secretaries:

Anne Carnt
Marina Hollis
Betty Linden

Pnina Steinmaz
Frances Whitehead

Summary

(i)   This report is about 2,367 accidents at work (both minor and serious) which occurred in four different types of industrial workshop over a period of between one and two years. It has been compiled from information recorded on the spot by trained observers who worked normal factory hours.

(ii)   The study was not aimed at fundamental discoveries about human behaviour but rather at the way in which what is already known can usefully be applied to the prevention of accidents in the industrial situation.

(iii)   The report shows the multiple nature of the factors which affect accidents, but many factors known to have an effect in the laboratory-type situation were barely perceptible in the four workshops.

(iv)   On the other hand, there is evidence to support the view that accidents are built into most industrial work and that changes in the design of the work will bring about a significant improvement in the accident rate.

(v)   There is also evidence that experience, even in the short-term, has a noticeable effect on accidents, and hence that operator training is worthwhile from the safety point of view, as well as from that of increasing production.

(vi)   A wider use of knowledge of ergonomic systems design is needed (including training and safety technology) in the design of systems of work in order to eliminate built-in accident factors. Courses are proposed for the safety specialist, and for the man whose basic discipline is engineering or design or management. It is suggested that for the latter, these courses can be introduced without enlargement of total syllabus, by substitution for matters of lower priority or by alteration of approach.

(vii)   In the meantime, much of what is known about how to modify existing systems of work to reduce risks, remains unapplied because communication between 'shop floor' and 'office' is ineffective.

(viii)   Safety departments do not overcome this problem because none of their personnel have jobs which keep them on the shop floor for long enough.

(ix)   The recommendation is that this problem be overcome by utilising the current legislative pressure towards industrial training. It is suggested that the logical connection between training and safety be made at all levels, so that shop floor trainers become the local members of the factory's safety organisation.

(x)   Communication between 'office' and 'shop floor', so far as training and safety is concerned, then becomes the job of the training-and-safety officer(s). His duty of supervision of the shop floor trainers should bring him on to the shop floor for a considerable proportion of his time, so that other contacts can be fostered.

(xi)   The Factory Inspectorate should extend its role to give a greater emphasis to teaching, as an encouragement to those concerned with shop floor training and safety. The increasing frequency of visits to factories which this implies would also demonstrate to management that government is concerned about industrial accidents.

(xii)   Some legislative changes are proposed, as a means of focusing attention on accident prevention, rather than on insurance and post-hoc blame-searching, and also as a means of improving the reliability of national statistics.

Preface

People who do research are open to two kinds of criticism. The first is that they may venture conclusions beyond the evidence as strictly recorded in the text of the report. The second is that they will not venture them.

In the kind of investigation that is reported here, which was beset by all the problems inherent in applied research carried out in real life situations, it was unlikely from the outset that there would be many clear cut and fully substantiated conclusions from statistical data alone. Indeed, the objects were exploratory: to formulate workable hypotheses even more than to test them. But the research team spent a total of about ten man-years in systematic and very detailed observation of everything that could be observed of the things that affect work on the shop floor and the people doing it and this has never been done before. They were bound to reach conclusions from their total experience which it would be stupid and wasteful to ignore.

Therefore, while taking pains to distinguish between what is verifiable and what should be classed as judgement, we have not hesitated to record judgement where it seemed to us important to the object of the research, namely, to prevent accidents.

R. B. BUZZARD,
Director, NIIP

Contents

CONTENTS

CONTENTS

Introduction

The Workshops

1 This report is about the accidents which we recorded in four different industrial workshops in the period 1966–69. The workshops were:

- a light assembly shop, with between 200 and 300 workers, mostly women. Some were working individually, but the majority were paced by conveyor belts;

- a machine shop, with between 100 and 200 workers of both sexes, but rather more men than women. The shop produced small pressings and a variety of small turned parts. The work was individual;

- a rolling mill, with between 100 and 200 workers, all men. This shop did short orders for strip metal. The work was by individuals or in pairs;

- a goods despatch department, with less than 100 workers, all men. Some of the work was individual but mostly it was done by groups of four or five.

Aims

2 The aims of the research are set out in the Appendices at para. 212 *et seq.* Briefly, it was to be an 'investigation on the shop floor, along inter-disciplinary lines, of environmental and personal factors contributing to accidents by methods which will permit the study of their interaction and combined effects'. This report attempts to put the accident scene of the individual factory or workshop into perspective and to indicate the directions in which efforts to improve industrial safety will produce the greatest results.

Method

3   The basis of the research method was continuous observation of each of the four shops by randomly patrolling observers who had definite tasks to do in the shops, but sufficient freedom to talk to and become thoroughly acquainted with every worker. We stayed in all shops for at least a year and in the first two, the assembly shop and the machine shop, we stayed nearly two years. The area occupied by each workshop was reasonably compact and we used a ratio of workers to observer of about 100:1.

Data collection

4   Most of the data we collected ourselves. Factory staff had insufficient time to do all we needed and, in general, factory records were insufficient for the details required by the research (see para. 220 *et seq.*). We gathered the data in four different ways. Environmental data, such as temperature and humidity, were continuously recorded by automatic apparatus; details of shop layout, machinery and such things as age and experience of people were gathered once in the first part of the observation period, and updated as necessary. Details of quickly changing things, such as who did what work, were recorded on a sampling basis, except at the despatch department, where the works records were sufficiently detailed and reliable to use them as a continuous record; accidents were recorded as and when they occurred, or were discovered by the observers.

What is an accident?

5   The definition of what we were to regard as an accident is given in para. 215. We took a note of everything which resulted in an injury, even if this was only a small cut to a finger, or a bruise to a shin. For every accident in the assembly shop and the machine shop, we also recorded comparable information from two people acting as controls, one matched for certain characteristics of the task he was doing at the relevant time and the other matched for personal characteristics of age, sex, and length of service (see para. 224 *et seq.*). In the mill, we were unsuccessful with controls, particularly the first, because most people were doing different tasks and we could not match the task characteristics. In the despatch department, there was sufficient homogeneity in the work for comparisons to be drawn with the whole population and separate controls were not used for each accident. For these reasons, different statistical techniques were used for the analysis of the mill and the despatch department, compared with those used for the assembly and machine shops.

Success and limitations of field method

6 We have shown that it is possible, with the co-operation of management and unions, for research workers to be introduced into a workshop, stay there for a year or two, and withdraw without any significant effect on the population concerned.

7 Attending a factory for purposes of friendly conversation and observation for eight hours, day after day, is not an occupation which appeals to many research workers. Some observers just cannot stand it; others are not acceptable to the population of the factory and these, if not detected at the selection stage, have to be diplomatically transferred into other work before they do any harm. The whole team found the observation periods too long. The ideal would have been about six months, but we could not have gathered the data we wanted in that time.

8 A ratio of one observer per 100 workers approximately was reasonably satisfactory in our shops where a lot of people were gathered in one area. Where workers are dispersed over larger areas, for example, on some building sites or works of engineering construction, it might be necessary to have two or more observers per 100 workers.

9 We investigated 2,367 accidents at work, obtaining the descriptions from the injured people. We carefully checked the descriptions with the details of the surroundings and concluded that what we were told was correct. There was no reason for anyone to withhold the truth from us, because we were not concerned with blame and our work was under a guarantee of confidence.

10 We recorded many more accidents than were recorded in first-aid room records but we know that occasionally we missed accidents where there were no visible signs of injury and some which were sustained by the more uncommunicative section of the population.

11 The research plan included the use of final interviews with employees. These were abandoned as we were satisfied that we would gain no more information in arranged interviews than we had already obtained in conversations during the period of observation.

12 Continuous observation of the practical situation has certain limitations. The observer has to live in the situation and therefore cannot do anything which might upset the people he is observing. Thus, it took some weeks after we were well known, to obtain permission from management, unions, and the individuals concerned to take some still photographs. The use of a cine camera would have been quite out of the question, because of its association with work study. We could not do anything which would interfere with production, because we undertook not to do so when we started the project. At the end of the project in the same factories, we probably could have mounted experiments which would have modified production, because, by that time, we had gained the confidence of all concerned. However, that would have been another project for which we had neither authority nor funds.

Time and cost

13   The work was originally planned to last five years. This was reduced to four to conform with the period for which a total grant of £45,000 was awarded. However, because of the delays in negotiations about shops which are perhaps inevitable in field research, it was not possible to complete the work in this time. It began in early 1966 and, to date, has taken five years at a total cost of about £74,000.

Findings

FACTORIES ACT 1961:-

Attitudes to accident prevention

14 The top managements of the firms concerned in this research were all keen about the promotion of safety in their factories. This was bound to be so, otherwise they would not have allowed us on their premises. Consequently, this report is about workshops with 'good' safety records. We found that the picture was not quite so good when we probed a little deeper but, even so, our firms were probably amongst the best.

15 The top management of a large firm does not often go walking round the workshops – it has other things to do. But neither did we find it sending its representatives to any appreciable extent. In three of our shops, the presence of a safety officer, a plant engineer or a designer was an event. In the fourth shop, we did not see it at all.

16 At shop floor level, there is often what appears to be an attitude of *acceptance* apathy towards safety matters. It amounts to acceptance of the *status quo*, in which many unsafe systems of work persist because their practice is established. For example, we regularly came across the dry turning of non-ferrous metals without eye protection for the operator, which shop supervision did not see as a breach of statute (S.65 of the Factories Act 1961).

see 59.

17 The attitudes of the workers themselves seemed to be that little could be done to prevent accidents. Operators handling sharp sheet steel pieces all day long accepted that they would receive minor cuts now and again. *attitudes of workers.* 'It's part of the job', they said. One particularly intelligent and adaptable man said, 'If you think about all the risks that go with this job, you'll drive yourself barmy'. Nevertheless, when we asked him to think about this, we found he did not fully appreciate some of the risks in his job (see para. 58).

18 We were interested by the acceptance of 'carelessness' as a cause of accidents amongst workers, supervisors and management at all our sites. Typical comments were: '90 per cent of accidents are caused by "carelessness" '; 'It was my fault, I was careless'. This belief in 'carelessness' as a unifactorial explanation of an accident, distracts attention from the many complex factors which contribute to the cause.

19 These attitudes seem to spring from two sources. First, the feeling that nothing effective can be done springs from ignorance. Here is an education and training problem, on the shop floor in the short term, and in the schools and colleges in the long term. At the end of this report we set out recommendations about this.

20 Secondly, there is a lack of contact and hence a gap in communication between the shop floor staff and the office administrators. Many risks on the shop floor remained because office staff did not know the problem existed; safety officers, for example, were unaware of several three-day lost time accidents; a dangerous jig was improvised instead of designed by a jig and tool specialist. In a similar way, labour turnover amongst certain sections of the shop population was a problem kept in the office, rather than investigated on the shop floor.

21 In other words, there is a 'we-they' relationship, apparently kept alive by geographical isolation and illusions of status. We have given this careful consideration, and our recommendations about the organisation of training and safety are an attempt to close the communication gap, at least so far as these two functions are concerned.

22 We think that attitudes must be changed if safety technology is to be effective in workshops. Two things are required:

(*a*) Management must be induced to take an interest and to look at what is really happening on the shop floor.

(*b*) Workers on the shop floor must be encouraged to feel that something ought to be done. Often it can. Shop floor safety representatives could encourage this, if they can be taught what to look for.

23 At one shop we came across a rumour about how injury claims were settled. Some people believed that if one was injured, one received damages as the result of a friendly haggle between the safety officer and the insurers. This misunderstanding of roles suggested that the unions were not instructing their members. We wondered if, in fact, some claims were settled by a chat between the safety officer and an insurance company representative. If this is what goes on, it is a sad state of affairs, which distracts the safety officer from his primary role.

Injury recording and first-aid facilities

24 We found a gross difference in the effectiveness of injury recording, depending on whether or not there was a fully staffed surgery associated with the workshop. Where this was the case, as at three of our shops, the surgery recorded between about 55 and 70 per cent of the injuries which we recorded. Where there was no fully staffed surgery, recorded accidents were about 5 per cent of the total we discovered. As far as the injuries leading to three days lost time were concerned, the shops with fully staffed surgeries recorded almost all of them, but the other shop recorded only about half of them.*

25 We did not find that propensity to report for treatment was related to the distance from the surgery. But no part of the shops with a surgery was any great distance from it, and the major part of the walk was indoors. A long walk outside in bad weather might well be off-putting to someone with a minor injury.

26 Other factors could have more marked effects on reporting. For example, in part of one shop, the work often involved holding a component with one hand near a revolving part of the machine, yet the surgery staff had sometimes dressed hand injuries with open-weave bandages which were prone to catch on the machine. If this happened, there was an excellent chance of a second, more serious, injury. The operators had a poor opinion of the surgery and they reported a lower proportion of their injuries than did other sections (see Appendix para. 233).

27 This last example shows one of the problems of communication to which we referred earlier. Here was a workshop operating an unsafe system of work; a surgery with a nurse who had no idea of dressings appropriate to the job; and neither organisation communicating its difficulties to the other.

---

* the lost injuries were recorded as 'sickness' or 'uncertificated absence'.

28 The first-aid facility at the workshop without a surgery was a small, locked room, with elementary first-aid equipment. Keys were held by trained first-aiders who were among the less heavily loaded members of the shop. Failure to record was partly because the first-aiders were not encouraged to use the notebook kept for the purpose in the first-aid room (no-one, apart from our observer, ever checked it, so far as we were aware), and partly because not all injuries were reported to, and treated by, the first-aiders.

29 The people at this shop who knew about most of the accidents were the first-aiders and the time-clerks but neither of these had the responsibility nor encouragement to record. (For details, see Appendix para. 241 *et seq.*)

30 Injury recording at one of the shops with a nearby surgery reached a higher standard – nearly 70 per cent of the total we observed. We understand that training of the surgery staff included a tour of the shops when intricacies of the work were explained. They seemed to be much more aware of their role; they were approachable and did not mind going across to the shop to have a look at things.

31 We concluded that industrial nurses must be taught about the hazards facing the workers in the shops they have to deal with. This must be done on the shop floor; it cannot be done only in a college of nursing, a hospital or some other factory. The nurses must go and see for themselves what is the situation special to their patients.

32 Proper records of injuries can be a useful pointer to the safety needs of a workshop but this requires records capable of analysis by workshop and possibly by sections of each workshop. Only one workshop had a system allowing this but, even there, the pointers did not appear to be drawn out and acted on. Reference to the Appendices, para. 256 *et seq.*, will show how lessons can be learned from examining the injuries inflicted by particular industrial processes. If the records can be extended by entering the agent of injury (i.e. the answer to the question 'what actually hit/cut you?'), there emerges a number of pointers for preventive action. For example, in our machine shop, this type of recording showed that flying swarf was more trouble than was generally realised on the lathes, and that the ancillary processes in the gear-cutting section caused more potentially serious trouble than the actual gear-cutting.

33 A note of warning. No-one must be deluded into thinking that surgery records can ever tell the whole story. They will tell a distorted story because full recording of all injuries is not possible in practice. For example, the peak accident day was Thursday at two of our shops according to the surgery records. But, in fact, we found that there were more accidents on Wednesday than on Thursday.

34 Finally, we noticed that new recruits did not report injuries so much as more experienced workers. A point for induction training and supervision?

The specific nature of each task

35 The longer we looked at a task in any of our workshops, the more we became impressed by the number of inherent risks of injury. If you work in an office, sitting at a desk, you can be reasonably certain that you will go home at the end of the day without so much as a scratch on you. Not so if you work at a lathe.

36 There you may cut your fingers on sharp material or components, lacerate the back of your right hand on the turret tools, blind your eyes with flying swarf, break your fingers or your arm by entanglement with revolving parts (this one has killed), or give yourself tenosynovitis by continual repetition of (awkward) bodily movements. If you go on working and there is oil about, you may develop oil dermatitis.

37 Further, the risk of your falling foul of these dangers is not constant throughout the day. In the morning, you may have dry work and flying swarf. In the afternoon, you may have wet work, with negligible eye risk but an increased dermatitis risk. If the turret is full of drills, you may very well cut the back of your right hand on one. If you are working mainly with the cross-slide, this risk is diminished. Each task carries its own risks and these are highly specific to the task. At all shops, we were able to show not only that people had different accident rates according to where they worked, but also according to precisely what tasks they performed in the course of that work. The accident rate varied from shop to shop, and from one section to another within any one workshop. Within a section, the accidents varied from one operator/machine combination to another and operator factors were difficult to separate from machine factors.

38 On any one machine, the accident rate depended largely on what class of component was worked; a change of component would result in a change of accidents, both in type and frequency. For example, turning brass produces flying swarf and eye injuries but turning mild steel seldom does this. However, if the steel is stainless, the swarf is stringy and sharp and there is a tendency for cut fingers. We found that even with the same component, a change of setter could precipitate an accident, because of subtle differences in the way he arranged the tools. And, to take it one stage further, we found on occasion that the changing of boxes of components could change the accident rate. This was because there were small dimensional differences in the components in the boxes which had produced some sharp edges in one but not in the next.

39   We had to contend with all these factors before considering what difference to the accident rate a change of operator might make. And, in fact, we could do this on a comparative basis to only a limited extent, as we could not disrupt production by swapping operators between machines and tasks to satisfy experimental requirements. Further, we could not reproduce batches of components which had already gone.

40   The despatch department was a better experimental situation. There we had groups of people doing an amount of work which was measurable from one day to the next. The mixture of various sorts of goods handled could be estimated with reasonable accuracy by sampling. Thus, we were able to examine the relationship between accidents and work done, and to see the effects of various types of goods and the various ways of handling them used by the men.

41   Thus, if we accept our shops as being typical of the industrial situation, the effect of subtle differences in machines and in components is to obscure the human causes of accidents and to make their separation from other factors extremely difficult. We conclude that it is invalid to compare one factory with another, one workshop with another, one section of a workshop with another, one machine operator with another or even one barrow pusher with another, without considering the specific nature of the range of risks involved. (For further details, see the Appendices, para. 280 *et seq.*)

Note: We have been impressed by the way small changes in the job, and the way it is arranged, can influence the accident rate. For this reason, we use the word 'task' to mean a particular set of operations done with a particular machine on a particular component. By 'work system', we mean the whole arrangement for getting the work done, which includes the people, the machines associated with their jobs, and the environment.

The need to design the systems of work

42 Over two-thirds of the injuries we observed were cuts on sharp edges. Most of these edges were on material or components but even parcels injured people. It struck us as absurd that a parcel, which is something wrapped for safe and convenient handling in transit, should have cutting edges. Yet in the despatch department, there were over 150 injuries of this type.

43 There appears to be a need for re-thinking about how to perform work. This was most noticeable in the machine shop, where the injury rate was highest. Many of the operators were doing little more than act like machines themselves, going through the same set of motions every minute or two (sometimes in less). If they made some aberration in the required movements, they often risked injury on a sharp edge. This might be something they were handling or a part of the machine itself. We even found a guard with a razor edge on it. Injuries in these circumstances were inevitable, in the long run. No-one can reproduce exactly the same movements, time after time. He may improve with practice but consistent repetition is achieved far better by a machine.

44 In this respect, many of the human tasks we were watching had parts which could have been done better by machine. In particular, the repeated insertion of components into machines was usually done manually although sometimes an additional mechanical feeder was employed. People were still doing these tasks because insufficient money and effort had been put into developing the extra machinery required. It was not considered worthwhile making a mechanical feeder that would be used only a few hours a week. (This is the argument used by highway authorities to avoid buying snow-clearing equipment.)

45 The complement of this argument is that machines are poor at doing things such as making decisions and recognising and correcting errors. These tasks are better done by people. Yet we saw batches of components, which had been badly machined on one process, proceeding through others and injuring the operators who handled them. Occasionally, complaints about injured fingers forced a decision to rectify a faulty batch. But making decisions was regarded as embarrassing and no-one was quite sure if he was entitled to do so. People were so busy behaving like automata that they could hardly cope when called on to do something human.

46   At a higher level, we knew a supervisor and two other skilled men who had identified a fault in a machine and decided to rectify it. This involved dismantling, but they went about this in the wrong way and one of them was seriously injured when the machine exploded. Here were men making decisions – a task at which men excel – but going wrong because they lacked knowledge and training.

47   Overall, there is a lack of recognition of the appropriate functions of machines and of people, and of systems which make use of the best from both of them. The need is for the design of all working arrangements with ergonomic principles in mind.

48   Re-thinking along new lines takes time. Meanwhile, there are short term remedies which hardly need an ergonomist to suggest them, although he might suggest better ones. For example:

– our parcel handlers needed gloves;

– the operators and others recognising faulty components needed an arrangement whereby their discovery could be acted upon and be seen as making a contribution to the quality of the product;

– the three skilled men needed to know when and where to seek help with unfamiliar machines. They could also have avoided the injury if they had been generally trained in dismantling charged apparatus by harmless methods.

Accidents and work done ('load effect')

49   The number of accidents appeared to be directly related to the amount of work people did. From our observations this seemed an obvious relationship, but it was difficult to establish statistically because of the large variety of tasks and change of risks (see the previous section on 'The specific nature of each task'). However, we were able to find a significant relationship for some groups, as shown below.

50   At the despatch department, the range of tasks was limited. We checked that the proportions of the different types of goods, with their different risks, were roughly constant, month by month. Hence, we assumed that an aggregate measure of department output reflected the total work done at constant risk. We found that the number of accidents per month was significantly related to the volume of parcels handled per month. On closer examination, we found that there were different accident rates for different tasks. People who handled a greater number of metal-banded parcels, sustained a greater number of injuries (from the bands).

51 In the more usual industrial situations of the assembly and machine shops and the rolling mill, we could not find a measure of output which took into account the changes of product mix and the consequent changes of risk. However, we did find that a sample chart of electricity consumed mainly by our machine shop, showed a higher current in the morning than in the afternoon. There were more accidents in the morning than in the afternoon at this shop.*

52 We examined the possibility of using bonus pay as a measure of work done per month. We thought that at least in one shop, where the work was unpaced, the effort a person put into his job ought to have been reflected in the bonus earned. But this was not true. On some tasks it was easy to earn a high rate of bonus, and, on others, it was difficult to earn even a modest bonus. On some of the more automated processes, the bonus earned was almost entirely governed by the machine speed and the operator could do little to increase his bonus earnings apart from seeing that the raw material supply was replenished and trust that the machine would not break down. We also discovered semi-official systems aimed at maintaining bonus earnings at a steady rate (for an example, see footnote to para. 128).

53 We came to the conclusion that simple and reliable measures of the human work content of a job are most difficult to find in a situation where the work is done by various combinations of man and machine, particularly when the men and machines change partners and change tasks every few hours. Nevertheless, the load effect seems to be present and is a useful way of explaining details of accident patterns. (For further details, see Appendix para. 307 *et seq.*)

* In an associated 2-year study of errors occurring in two particular jobs in one industry, we found that the peaks and troughs of the curve of error against time-of-day, corresponded with those of the curve of number of operations performed.

Experience of the worker

54 We found that accidents decreased as worker experience increased. We had three measures of experience:

(a) *Length of service.* At three shops, we could demonstrate that accidents decreased in frequency as the length of service increased. At the fourth, so few people had short service that the relationship could not be studied.

(b) *Frequency of repetition of task.* People repeating a task, which they had done in the recent past, had less accidents on it than on tasks which they did only occasionally. People who changed tasks frequently had more accidents than those who did not change frequently.

(c) *Time on the task.* On a quickly repetitive task, the highest accident rate occurred towards the beginning of the period on the task.

55 We think the above is an illustration of the learning theory of behaviourist psychology. If a task has risks of injury built into it, people doing the task eventually learn how to avoid these risks for most of the time. They learn and retain methods of avoiding risks which are common to the generality of all the tasks they have to do, but the lessons learned about risks which are peculiar to one particular task are retained for only a few days, and, if that task does not recur, the lesson fades. If the task eventually recurs, some re-learning must be done.

56 It follows that new recruits to a factory will have a higher accident rate than people who have been there for some time. We found that recruitment and accidents were significantly related at the two shops where recruitment was appreciable.

57 We conclude that training which embraces the techniques of risk-avoidance specific to the tasks in hand, would be a way of reducing accidents, especially amongst recruits.

Statistical details are given in the Appendix, para. 339 *et seq.*

Seeing the risk

58 An exploratory study in two of the shops showed that the risks an individual sees in his job are mainly those to which he has succumbed himself or to which his neighbours have succumbed (see Appendix para.

363 *et seq.*). This implies a lack of teaching about the risks of a job and how to avoid them.

59 Many people accepted small cuts and scratches as an inevitable part of industrial life and were not bothered by them. This lack of concern about minor injuries can lead to lack of concern about their causes and herein lies a danger that some major risk is overlooked. However, this line of thought must not be taken too far. Some tasks carry the risk of minor injury only, some of major injury only and some have risks of both. Repetition of minor injury is a warning of major injury only in certain cases: e.g. eye injuries from flying swarf – see Appendix para. 381 *et seq.*

Training

60 We have no measures of training or its effectiveness, but the lack of it is implied in the section on Experience. The common form of job training was 'sitting with Nellie', assisted by a little intermittent instruction from a chargehand, a machine setter, or a foreman.

61 In one shop, a new recruit would sit beside an experienced operator and gradually take over the task in the course of several days. There were one or more 'reject' operators to each group, whose job was to put right any defective work. These reject operators were people of long experience on all the tasks. If they found a fault recurring several times, they were supposed to go to the chargehand who would put the matter right with the appropriate operator. Sometimes the reject operator went directly to the operator and showed her how to avoid the fault. The reject operators thus functioned as trainers. When the factory started a training section, to satisfy the requirements of the Industrial Training Act, we suggested that, at least as an interim measure, some reject operators could be promoted to trainers. This was adopted, apparently with success.

62 At another shop, operators sometimes instructed new recruits, but more usually the instruction was by a setter (and occasionally by a foreman). He would demonstrate the task, watch the recruit do it a few times, correct errors and, thereafter, visit from time to time to check that all was well. Some machining tasks are frightening to the uninitiated, and many require considerable dexterity. We noticed some cases where the training was insufficient for recruits without comparable experience. These individual cases had high accident rates and either left the factory altogether or transferred to another workshop.

63   At a third shop, labour turnover was low. New recruits were trained by being placed fifth or sixth person in an established group. Instruction in the rudiments of the task was given by other members of the group. In general, this instruction was little and random. We visited another shop doing the same kind of work and found a special training group consisting of four people who were considered by the management to be 'good, safe workers'. We do not know what criteria the management used in this consideration.

64   At the fourth shop, turnover was also low but again training was mostly 'sitting with Nellie'. One new assistant operator was trained by the operator he assisted. An operator upgraded from assistant was trained by another who came to work on his machine for a while. There was a scheme of training for truck drivers, which involved a special works-based course lasting several days. Although no new truck drivers were employed during our observation period, there were some learner drivers who were working before going on the training course. One of these drivers was a learner for two years and was involved in an accident during this period.

65   The general pattern of training we saw was haphazard and often carried out by people who did not know how to train. Although some of these people were quite good at the tasks themselves, they could not teach them properly to others because they did not understand how to teach; they had no system of instruction. We conclude that on-the-job training could be much more effective if it was done by people who had been trained to train.

Recruitment and allocation to jobs

66   The two shops where labour turnover was a serious problem were in areas where competition for labour with neighbouring factories was high. The workshop population consisted of a 'core' of people (just over half the establishment), who stayed there for the whole of our observation period, and a fringe of people who changed quite frequently. The personnel department could not do much more than allocate people to jobs in the shops that needed labour.

67   The recognition of suitable or unsuitable people was virtually left to the setters in one of these shops and to the operators in the other. Induction training of recruits was part of their job, although it did not seem to be officially recognised as such and they had no training in how to teach the skills required. So it took a week or two before a worker unsuited to the task was recognised as such and a transfer arranged. A properly experienced trainer should be able to recognise at least the extreme examples of such people in a few hours' instruction, and could be given authority to re-allocate the worker to more suitable tasks.

68 Recruits sustain accidents because of their lack of experience (see Appendix para. 342 *et seq.*). One section of our machine shop was short of women operatives on several occasions and it seemed that almost anyone who was willing to have a go would be sent there. One recruit who was particularly ham-fisted and frightened of the machines, quickly suffered injury and had a narrow escape from a serious accident before she was offered transfer to an assembly job and took it. This was not in an area we were watching but we understand she managed in her new job quite happily.

Cost of accidents

69 Taking our four shops as a whole, the number of man-hours lost through accident was roughly equivalent to the permanent absence of four people. The total wages cost was in the region of £3,500 per annum, and if one assumes the labour content of a factory product to be 20 per cent, the equivalent product sales loss is £16,500 per annum. To a large factory this is peanuts, and is no doubt one of the reasons why accidents are not regarded as a serious problem.

70 However, the cost of accidents is not simply accountable, and is not a burden on the factory so much as on the community. A factory may have a first-aid service included in its on-costs, but the community has a hospital service, a national insurance scheme, and a legal service to pay for, thus relieving the factory of further responsibility for the people it maims. The factory produces goods and injuries; the community at large pays for both.

Distribution of accidents month-by-month

71 All our shops showed a variation in the accident rate, from one month to another (see Appendix para. 444 *et seq.*). The explanation appears to lie in variations in the amount of work done and in changes of worker experience.

72 At the despatch department, with its stable population, the numbers of accidents per month were significantly related to the volume of parcels handled.

73   At the mill, which again had a stable population, an increase in accidents was related to an increase in work-load and more overtime.

74   At the other two shops, labour turnover was fairly high. Recruitment varied with the demands of the trade. For example, in the winter of 1966-67 during the trade recession, recruitment stopped. In the following months there was a big recruitment drive as trade improved. Thus, there were widely varying intakes of inexperienced workers and this was reflected in the number of accidents sustained (see Appendix para. 342 *et seq.*).

Distribution of accidents over the days of the week
75   We looked at the accident rate on different days of the week because so many people asked us about 'Black Monday'.

76   We found that there were only two factors appearing to affect the pattern of accidents over the days of the week. These were the work-load and the absence. Work-load was difficult to measure comparatively and only at the despatch department were we really successful. In the other workshops our measures were partial or subjective.

77   The work-loads in our shops were different. In two, there was generally an ample supply of work at all times during the week and the amount of work actually done, per day, appeared at first sight to be a matter of social custom. People told us that they preferred to work hardest on Monday, Tuesday and Wednesday. Thursday was pay-day, Friday was the start of the weekend and no-one reckoned to work particularly hard on those two days. At another shop, the first four days of the week seemed to be quite busy and people only relaxed a little on Friday, which was pay-day.

78   Superimposed on the effect of work-load is that of absence. In this study, we found that absence was highest on Mondays and lowest on pay-days, with intermediate days graduated between these extremes.* On Monday, when absence is high, more than usual of those who come to work have to tackle an unfamiliar task, or work with unfamiliar colleagues,

* This is commonly found but many different patterns can exist in different factories or departments within factories.

in order that the more essential work gets done. Thus, the increased absence causes an increase in the inexperience effect and an increase in the accident rate.

79 So the pattern we find over the days of the week, for accidents per head of attendant population, is that Monday is universally a high day and that the rate thereafter is more or less steady until the bonus account is made up. Then the accident rate drops.

80 However, at the despatch department, everyone worked straight through the week and there was no significant difference in the daily work-load. This was strikingly at odds with what we found in the other three shops and appeared to have been caused by a difference in the way bonus was calculated. At the despatch department, it was calculated daily, on the tonnage moved each day. Thus, each day was a fresh start and the bonus for that day had to be earned by work done that day. At the other three shops, bonus was calculated weekly, so that people could make up for taking it easier one day by working harder on another. There was only one fresh start per week, this being on Thursday morning at the assembly and machine shops and on Friday at the mill.

81 Daily bonus accounting is impracticable in most industrial work. If it is to be done weekly, then it seems best to make a fresh start every Monday morning. This would help to keep the work-load steady. We doubt if it would eliminate an 'end of the week' effect, but this could be better confined by paying on Friday. (Housewives and local traders would no doubt object to this, because it would squeeze more shopping into Saturday. Bank or Giro accounts seem to be the answer.)

Further details are given in the Appendices, para. 449 *et seq.*

Distribution of accidents over the hours of the day
82 The distribution of accidents over the hours of the day had three characteristics. First, the accident rate is higher in the morning than in the afternoon and the peak time for accidents occurs after mid-morning. This pattern occurred generally and we think it is a reflection of the work-load.

83 Secondly, superimposed over the first effect, there were localised peaks of accidents occurring before breaks. This appeared to be mainly the effect of target-setting by the operators. It was more marked in the machine shop where work was individual, than in the assembly shop where the work was belt-paced. At the mill, the operators told us that they set themselves targets to achieve before the next break.

84 We thought these peaks might also be due in part to increasing variability of performance after the first hour or so of the task, as postulated by Murrell (1965). A special study of four lathe operators in our machine shop, carried out by an M.R.C. ergonomist (see Appendix para. 505 *et seq.*) revealed that this effect appeared to be there but the operators themselves offset it by frequent changes of activity, such as stopping to light a cigarette, to chat or getting up to fetch a new box of components.

85 Thirdly, at the end of the afternoon, the peak of accidents was either non-existent or was less pronounced and preceded a decline, as people stopped work to tidy up before going home.

86 At the despatch department, the decline was particularly noticeable because it was an established shop practice to stop work $\frac{1}{4}$ to $\frac{1}{2}$ hour before the end of a shift, to wash and change. But so far as the late shift was concerned, there was a marked peak in the penultimate half-hour, which was one of the busiest periods of the day.

87 Of the other three shops, we expected the best defined peak in the assembly shop, because the conveyor belts, pacing the work, were run to within a few minutes of the end of the shift. But we found the machine shop still showed the most peak; the assembly shop and the mill showed negligible peak (Further details are given in the Appendix para. 483 *et seq.*).

Temperature and humidity
88 In the assembly shop, most of the work was done sitting down. The shop was centrally heated and temperatures ranged from 17°C in the extremes of winter to over 25°C on hot summer afternoons.

89 In the machine shop, conditions were similar but more of the work was done standing up. In both shops, however, workers walked about comparatively little.

90 We found that significantly more accidents occurred at temperatures below about 20°C in both these shops. There was no similar upper boundary but this was almost certainly due to the noticeable slackening of work done in hot weather.

91 In the despatch department, most of the work involved energetic movements and much walking about, sufficient to keep people comfortable at lower temperatures. This shop was unheated and had sides open to the atmosphere in several places. Temperatures ranged from −5°C to 30°C. We found that accidents were at a minimum in the range 10°–15°C, but this was a tendency rather than a statistically significant result.

92 The mill had conditions midway between those of the first two shops and those of the despatch department. Much of the work was moderately energetic, and temperatures ranged from 11°C–28°C. There was no relationship discernible between accidents and temperature.

93 Vernon (1936) and others have shown that industrial accidents increase above and below a fairly narrow range of temperature, and experimental studies have shown similar effects on deterioration of perception. These effects may be obscured in the industrial situation by various factors. For example, at the despatch department, most of the men wore gloves in the colder weather and were thereby protected from the hand injuries which form the bulk of the injuries recorded over the year. In hot weather, the men stripped off and were thus able to keep themselves reasonably cool in temperatures which would have been uncomfortable to a factory worker compelled by social custom to wear a shirt and overall.

94 Humidity seemed to have little effect. In the machine shop, there was a tendency for more accidents at the extremes of humidity. Only in the assembly shop did significantly more accidents occur at humidities below about 50 per cent. (This is an odd result in view of the lack of correlation between accidents and high temperature; low humidity usually goes with high temperature. However, it is not an exact relationship.)
   The Appendix para. 548 *et seq.*, give further details.

Noise
95 We had a range of noise levels in our shops from the comparatively quiet (70 dB) during which conversation was easy without raising the voice, to the unpleasantly noisy (100 dB) where conversation was almost impossible. We cannot say what effect on accidents this variation had, because both accidents and noise are associated with particular work processes (for example, press work or shearing). We could not compare the same jobs under both quiet and noisy conditions (see also the Appendix para. 563).

EAR PLUGS.

96 Some parts of two of our shops had noise levels which would produce hearing loss in the course of time. Our observers used ear plugs of special quality glass wool imported from Sweden and found this most effective. We introduced this wool to several people in the noisy part of the shops and most of them liked it. We asked the surgery staff if they thought it was a good idea to stock it and they said they did. But we did not see it thereafter. We think the idea would probably have spread if the safety officer had assisted with it.

97 In general, the medical and safety staffs were concerned about the high noise levels in some parts of the shops. Although no-one in the shops seemed worried, several people expressed their dislike of the continual din. We noticed that some of the more modern press tools had been designed to produce less impact noise. We thought more could be done by screening and by mounting machines on attenuators. We think noise legislation is overdue.

Personal factors

98 We found personal characteristics had very few significant effects. We looked at such personal characteristics as age, sex, height, weight, marital status, number of dependants, distance and method of travel to work, medical history and intelligence. We found that none of them correlated with accidents, except at the despatch department, where men with a height of less than 5′ 9″ had significantly more accidents than the big fellows.

99 Accidents were found to be related to age at two of the shops but the relationships were contradictory in different groups of people. We could not control for both task and experience when looking at age. It seems that the effects of task and experience are more important than age.

100 We gave an extraversion/introversion test to samples of people at all shops and found that extraversion scores correlated with accidents in two of them. However, we also found that people who talked to us more had more accidents, according to our records (including accidents at home). We concluded that 'chattiness' might be the underlying cause of the relation between extraversion and recorded accidents.

101 In case anyone is tempted to try weeding out accident repeaters by a test of extraversion or some judgement about how talkative they are, we add three warnings. First, several of our accident repeaters were adaptable people who did a lot of work on a variety of (sometimes extraordinary) tasks. Their removal from the section would have been a considerable loss. Second, our 'chatty' people often made a valuable contribution to the morale of the working group. Third, we did not find a high individual accident score necessarily indicated a propensity for serious accident, although it certainly merited an examination of the work, to find the reason for the high score.

The Appendix para. 567 *et seq.*, deals with all the personal factors which we studied.

Absence and lateness

102 Some researchers have proposed that the types of people who have high numbers of accidents are those who exhibit certain patterns of absence behaviour.

103 At two shops, there was a significant relationship between accidents and uncertificated absence but this did not hold good in a third. In the fourth, data were not available. We found, in the first two shops, that it was the younger people who had significantly more uncertificated absence. Since the younger people were least experienced, we thought the relationship between accidents and uncertificated absence arose from both being a function of experience and age.*

104 There was no general pattern connecting lateness and accidents except in one shop, where the younger people were more often late and had more accidents.

105 There was no relationship between certificated absence and accidents at any of our shops. The certificated absence contained some absence directly caused by accidents, so we extracted this and examined the relationship between the remaining certificated absence (which was caused by sickness) and accidents. There was no relationship. This contradicts some previous research findings.

Further detail is to be found in the Appendix para. 621 *et seq.*

Sleeping, eating and tiredness

106 Over the course of about 1,000 accidents in the assembly shop and

---

* i.e. accidents are related to experience: experience is related to age: and uncertificated absence is related to age.

the machine shop, we made enquiries about the previous night's sleep and found that there was a tendency for accident victims to have had less sleep than their controls.

107 In general, we found no relationship between accidents and meals despite the fact that there were differences in eating habits between our various groups of workers.

108 We thought substantial physical tiredness would occur towards the end of the day at the despatch department and we collected a number of comments from workers to this effect. However, we could not trace an increase in accidents caused by tiredness and we think the effect was swamped by that of work-load.

109 The drop in accidents towards the end of the day at the other three shops corresponded with a general decline of work activity which could partly be ascribed to tiredness.

Further detail is to be found in the Appendix para. 629 *et seq.*

Home accidents

110 It was not intended that we take detailed notes of accidents sustained outside work, but we recorded as many as we heard about. There were about 330 and they resulted in about 1,500 hours lost work. The Health Education Council Ltd are carrying out a field study of enquiry into the causes of home accidents in Bristol. It appears to be well worth doing.

Monotony

111 A few people mentioned monotony to us but this was not widely acknowledged as a problem. Several people on repetitive work said they were bored when they had a much longer than usual run on a task, but, in general, an outsider may be misled as to the monotonous life of a factory.

There is however great scope for job enlargement and enrichment in industry.

112 Periods of boredom with a task can be tolerated more easily in an enjoyable social setting yet the latter is seldom deliberately encouraged by management. There were several groups in our workshops where the social ties were strong and the change of personnel was small. We witnessed the disintegration of one such group when a member was sacked. He had been an important part of the social structure and the group was unable to survive without him. We wondered if management fully realised the damage done by such things as this. We knew several other people who left their jobs because they were moved away from their friends in the workshop.

Alcohol

113 The work at the despatch department was generally of a heavy nature. About a quarter of the men had a drink regularly at local pubs during their lunch break and many more went to a pub occasionally. The practice was increased by warm weather.

114 There were several men who always drank more than two pints of beer at lunchtime, but these men did not feature significantly in the high accident score group.

High and low accident scorers

115 In each workshop we compared a sample of the high accident scorers with a sample of the low accident scorers, controlling for section and for job, where appropriate. We found that high scorers exhibited one or more of the following characteristics. Cases were observed in all workshops (except where shown), and confirmed statistically in at least one workshop:

(a) They had a shorter length of service (not at the despatch department)

(b) they did a larger variety of task (not apparent at the mill)

(c) they talked to us more (not at the despatch department)

(d) they had a higher extraversion score (statistical relationship nil at the assembly and despatch)

(e) they worked more on tasks which we classified as carrying a high risk. (This classification was subjective, but based on systematic study of the work and our general industrial experience.)

116 The above five characteristics (four, if you accept that (c) and (d) are the same in practical terms) were the only ones we felt could be described as generalities. Other characteristics either showed inconsistencies (e.g. age – see Appendix para. 569 et seq.), or inter-relationships with a third factor (e.g., uncertificated absence – see Appendix para. 103). We should perhaps add that we knew several high accident scorers who had a high capacity for work; several more who employed poor work methods, and the odd one or two of apparently low intelligence or infirmity from age. These latter 'oddities' seemed to us to be patent cases for transfer to harmless, simple or sitting-down jobs.

117   At one shop overtime was worked, and we found a tendency for high accident people to do more overtime than low accident people (see Appendix para. 643 *et seq.*).

118   We do not regard the relationship between accidents and 'chattiness' (or extraversion) as meaning more than that chatty people tend to report accidents, by whatever means is available, to a greater extent than do the non-communicative people. The non-relationships in the team atmosphere of the despatch department and, to a lesser extent in the assembly, reinforce us in this view. In other words, high or low accident scoring can be explained in terms of the details of the work done and the particular experience of the worker.

119   H. M. Vernon (1936) saw in repeated injuries the need to transfer the worker concerned to some other occupation where the risks of injury were less. We do not take this narrow view. We see repeated injuries as a pointer for various kinds of actions. That action may be re-allocation to another job, but may also be modifications of the work, or the re-training of the worker. A decision about these cannot be made from looking at records out of their context. Someone knowledgeable about the work must go and look at it, see how the injuries are arising and choose appropriate preventive measures.

Major and minor accidents

120   If we define a major accident as one which involves the injured party in absence from work for three days or more, then the proportion

Table 1

	Ratio, minor/major
Despatch department	15
Rolling mill	43
Machine shop	54
Assembly shop	412

of major to minor accidents was small. It varied from workshop to workshop in a way we expected, because the work at one place patently carried different risk of serious injury to that at another. The figures are given in the table on previous page.

121 Some people claim that individual records of minor injury indicate a propensity for that individual to have a major accident. However, we found that minor and major accidents were related only amongst one section of the population of one workshop (the despatch department).

122 We had a small number of major accidents and the findings above may not be representative. However, we would not expect a statistical connection because we found that the agent and type of injury in a major accident were often different from that of a minor one; often different risks were involved (see Appendix para. 390 *et seq.*).

123 Viewed in this light, the correlation amongst the group at the despatch department was probably the result of their job being a fairly homogeneous mixture of handling and walking about. The risks associated with both these activities were present most of the time. In our other shops, the risks changed with each task change.

124 Our overall impression of the major accidents is that most of them featured the victim coming across something which he had met infrequently, perhaps never before. He then made an inappropriate response to the situation. Inexperience can therefore be accounted a factor.

MAJOR ACCIDEN CAUSED BY THE UNKNOWN.

125 Training in an appropriate response would be one way of avoiding the accident but if the dangerous situation occurs infrequently, the victim may forget what he has learned and either not recognise the situation, or forget the appropriate response. So training for a rare situation requires regular reinforcement. This may be inconvenient and a better way of avoiding accidents would be a redesign of the work system to eliminate the dangerous situation.

Bonus pay
126 All our workshops operated pay schemes under which workers' wages consisted of a fixed part and a variable part, which depended on some measure of product output, such as the number produced in a given

time. Whether or not bonus pay correlated with accidents depended on what measure of product output was used for its calculation.

127   For example, in one shop, bonus was paid on weight. Accidents were related to weight, for the shop as a whole (but not to an extent which was statistically significant). Hence, there was some relationship between bonus and accidents, for the shop as a whole. But, on looking at individual groups of people, the bonus some groups earned was not related to accidents because some groups had consistently heavy but low-risk loads, so that they earned high bonus but had few accidents (see Appendix para. 324).

128   In another shop, bonus was paid on pieces produced per hour over a pre-set number. In this case bonus pay did not correlate with accidents (see Appendix para. 310). There were two reasons for this. First, a count of pieces of product per hour is not a measure of the human work involved in production, when the effort of production is shared between a person and a machine. Second, shop floor personnel (supervisors, clerks and operators) worked a system which tended to even out piece-work earnings between one task and the next and between one week and the next.*

129   The bonus pay schemes appeared to affect the distribution of accidents day-by-day according to whether bonus was made up daily or weekly. A weekly account allows more scope for varying the individual work effort throughout the week according to choice.

130   In the general industrial situation, bonus pay is unlikely to correlate with accidents, because there are few cases where it properly reflects the human work content of the task.

Malingering and exaggeration of injuries
131   We saw only three cases of injury where there was some question of malingering. Two of them involved spinal strains. One man told our observer he felt like having a week off but this was fairly obviously meant as a joke. He had strained his back and received medical attention. We took

---

* Tasks were 'good' or 'bad' according to the ease with which high bonus could be earned. In the records of work done, there was a tendency for the hours taken on a good task to be extended and on a bad task to be reduced in compensation. Records of bonus earned by individuals weekly were scanned by considerate supervisors, who then tried to arrange good jobs for those with low bonus in a preceding week.

his remark as a humorous way of saying that he did not feel fit enough to work. Another man was thought of by his colleagues as a malingerer when he was away from work for some considerable time with a spinal injury. But towards the end of this time, we saw him make a social visit to the workshop wearing a collar support. We concluded that if his medical advisers had made him go to those lengths, then he probably would have been in difficulties attempting to do his normal work. He applied for light work but was told that nothing was available.

132 The third case involved a head injury. The man was absent for a long time and he received specialist treatment at a hospital. The absence was certificated. One or two people in the shop suggested that this man was taking longer to recover than he need have done. We saw no foundation for these remarks. Pay at his shop was relatively good and anyone having to exist on National Insurance payments would find life particularly hard.

133 The members of our working populations, roughly 1,000 people including those who came and went in the years we watched, did not, to our knowledge, make any untoward fuss about their injuries. Indeed the reverse was true of three people at one shop, who injured themselves at home in ways that could very well have been blamed on their work, but who nevertheless made no attempt to associate the injury with it.

134 Malingering may be seen as a problem by those who deal with serious injuries but these are a tiny part of the accident spectrum. In our workshops, in 2,367 injuries, malingering was of no significance at all.

Removal of guards
135 We have often heard the idea expressed that operators remove guards from their machines and thereby lay themselves open to injury. The concept embraces breach of Section 143 of the Factories Act 1961. We kept a special eye open for this practice, but saw none for which the operator of the machine could be held responsible.

136 We had a case of a supplementary guard left off a grinding wheel after maintenance, apparently because the maintenance fitter did not think it worth re-fitting. We had cases of drill guards not fitted by setters when they could very well have been. This was a matter of established practice. On lathes with stock bar tubes, the gap between the end of the tube and the head stock of the lathe was enclosed, but the enclosure had a hinged flap through which access could be obtained to the bar when necessary. Some of these hinged flaps were in the raised position when we arrived at the shop and they were observed in a similar position at frequent intervals in the following 21 months. There was nothing by way of lock, inter-lock or established practice to keep them down. There were no injuries of any kind at this point and people did not see this as a risk.

Safety clothing

137 In some ways, the need for safety clothing is an admission of defeat. It ought to be possible to design a system of work where the protection of the worker does not depend on what he wears. However, this is an ideal yet to be achieved in many processes.

138 Our industries left the issue of safety clothing largely to the discretion of the shop supervisors, who did not often appreciate what was required. Thus, our goods handlers worked without gloves except in very cold weather, when many provided their own. Impermeable aprons were issued to people working oily lathes, but no spectacles to protect the eyes from flying swarf (until we raised the point with the safety department).

139 We heard of the niggardly attitude of some supervisors towards the issue of items which wore out fairly quickly, such as gloves. It was as though they had to pay for the clothing themselves! In fact, there seemed to be a grain of truth in this; we understood that safety equipment was accounted as a shop on-cost, so foremen might see it as something to be economical about. It would be better for accountants to charge safety to the factory as a whole.

140 The appearance of personal safety clothing is often overlooked. We think it important that it should be good looking, so far as is consistent with function. It is better to provide 80 per cent protection which people will wear than 99 per cent protection which will not be worn because it is ugly. (See Appendix para. 646 *et seq.*)

Established practice

141 The concept of 'established practice' occurs in legal cases brought as a result of injuries sustained at work. If the Court finds that the worker has been injured partly or wholly as a result of his pursuing a practice which he knew or ought to have known was dangerous, he can defend himself against allegations of negligence by showing that what he did was the normal practice in the premises in which he was employed. The aim of the injured party is to turn the tables and show that the dangerous practice was established to the extent that the employer or his supervising agent knew or should have known about it.

142 We found several dangerous practices firmly established. For example: the insertion and removal of components from the running collet of a lathe; the use of a cotton glove permanently worn on the hand as a convenient means of transferring oil from an open tin to the surface of strip metal feeding into a power press. The former carried a risk of injury to the fingers which materialised in several accidents on the lathes; the latter carried a serious risk of dermatitis which did not materialise during our observation, but may well do so in time.

143 The lesson for the safety department is that constant vigilance is required on the shop floor by people who can recognise dangerous practices and see that they are corrected. The supervisors we knew may have been vigilant and they had the power to make alterations of practice but they did not recognise the dangers. Our safety officers would have recognised the dangers if they had stopped, looked and thought about it, but they were not on the shop floor for long enough. In fact, they were hardly ever there.

Supervision

144 We had no direct measures of the effectiveness of supervision, but our observers gained the impression that supervisors (and setters) were not really alive to the need for a constant effort to improve operator safety. There was apathy and lack of knowledge. The Factory Inspectorate, the employers' federations and RoSPA all publish pamphlets about particular risks in particular trades but none of our observers ever saw any of this literature in any part of any of our workshops.

145 Supervisors and setters can influence accident rates through leadership, in our opinion. When we persuaded a safety department to introduce good looking safety spectacles for lathe operators in one shop, the supervisors and setters did not set an example by wearing them. After a few months, some operators stopped wearing them but no action was taken and hence the safety habit waned.

146 We noticed machine setters would set up the same task in subtly different ways, e.g. one man arranged the tools closer to the work than another, so that the operator cut his hand by accidental contact with the tools.

147 One of us devised a simple chip deflector, for a task on a lathe, which prevented splinters being thrown towards the operator's face. The setter used it once or twice, then mislaid it and did not bother again.

148 We devised a guard for a task which involved offering up a component to a grinding wheel. The guard was effective in preventing accidental contact of the operator's knuckles with the moving grindstone. When the wheel was changed on routine maintenance, the guard was not refitted. Neither the foreman, the shop steward nor the setter bothered to see that it was refitted although all of them had seen it and agreed that it was a worth-while arrangement.

149 Supervision can also affect the distribution of accidents. For example, in one shop, some foremen directed 'plum jobs' towards certain groups. These were tasks which paid a high bonus but they also involved fewer risks. Consequently, these favoured groups had fewer accidents, at the expense of other groups who had more (see Appendix para. 662.)

150 We thought supervisors could do more about safety if they were better trained in what to look for. They could anticipate more of the risks in the work done on their section. They could divert high risk work from inexperienced operators (some do this but not all). They could set a better example. They could be much more knowledgeable. Of course, supervisors could probably say that higher management is not knowledgeable and does not set them an example either. Shop floor supervisors are up against the 'communication gap' (see para. 20) and we think their position is unenviable.

Safety Committees

151 Our experience of safety committees was limited, but it seems to us fairly obvious that they will be effective only if there are means for carrying out their recommendations, and willingness on the part of both management and workers to co-operate. The three essentials are interested management representatives, practical suggestions and a proper follow-up to see that they are carried out.

152 One shop did have a safety committee and we thought that the good housekeeping in the shop was a reflection of its work. We understood that the recommendations of the committee were followed up by the shop manager and this was effective in getting decisions implemented.

153   At two of the shops, there were no safety committees as such but the factory had a committee of union representatives and management. This met at regular intervals and matters of safety could be raised at these meetings. We did not succeed in being invited to more than one introductory session of this committee. We gained the impression that matters of safety referred to the committee were foisted on to the shoulders of the safety officer, who appeared to be kept so busy dealing with serious accidents and the claims arising from them, that his effort on other things could only be spread thinly.

154   One shop did not have a resident safety officer. The management/ union committee discussed safety amongst other items, but management was apathetic about some matters and appeared unable to expedite others on which agreement had been reached. There was a breakdown of effective communication here, not only between shop floor and the office, but also between one office and another, i.e. the management and the maintenance department, and between both of them and the safety department.

Propaganda

155   We mentioned in the section on Supervision, that safety propaganda in the form of Factory Inspectorate booklets and so on was not to be seen in our workshops. Much the same can be said of other forms of propaganda. The occasional poster of general exhortation appeared now and again on notice boards, but that was all. There was a Safety Week at two shops, involving an exhibition nearby but it had no observable or measurable effects.

156   In our view, safety propaganda misses its mark because the people who devise and distribute it do not have regard for the high degree of specialisation in the workshop. A man who spends his time operating a capstan lathe is not the slightest bit interested in looking at a poster while he is on his way to lunch telling him to lash his ladder securely. He needs a poster right opposite his machine, warning him about eye risks and showing him an attractive, fashionable design of safety spectacle. Even this message is better conveyed by the foreman or a shop floor trainer who can see that the message gets home and who can reinforce the lesson if it is disregarded.

157   Our overall impression of safety propaganda is that it does not reach the people who need it when they need it. Consequently, when matters of safety were discussed, we found areas of gross misinformation or ignorance.

158   We view with distrust safety competitions with prizes for fewest accidents. Any social pressure which tends to dissuade people from recording their injuries will produce an artificial reduction in recorded injury rate (see, for example, para. 26).

Legislation

159   The effect of legislation was impossible to measure but we did see the Power Presses Regulations, 1965, come into effect. We were impressed by the added attention thereby given to proper function of the guards in the press section of the machine shop. However, this section was by no means a bad one before the Regulations came into force. The Regulations had no effect on the accident rate, so far as we could see, because no-one fell foul of the few remaining loopholes during that period of our observation before the Press Inspector started work. However, the new standard of care which he initiated would have prevented at least one nasty accident which we heard had taken place in the period before our observations started. We think the overall effect of the Regulations can be nothing but good, particularly on the incidence of serious accidents.

160   Appendix 31 (para. 665 *et seq.*) deals in more detail with our observations on compliance with various sections of the Factories Act 1961. Our overall impression was that, broadly, statute was complied with but knowledge of the detailed requirements was rare on the shop floor. Bearing in mind the complexities of interpretation of, for example, Section 14, this is hardly surprising. Nevertheless, in relation to some of the quite complicated technical knowledge which supervisors have of certain processes, we believe it is possible to teach shop floor personnel more about the technical requirements of those sections of the Factories Act which affect them in their own work. The failure of propaganda and information services generally is relevant here and is linked with the lack of training. The unions could help but are their official publications written in language intelligible to shop floor personnel? See 'The Injured Workman' by Voce (G. & M.W.U. 1969) which introduces the words 'negligence ' and 'liability' in their legal sense without any attempt at definition. It is a nice little summary for a well-educated law student.

Legal penalties

161 If a man loses his arm in an unfenced dangerous machine at a factory, the occupier may be prosecuted in the criminal courts and fined up to a maximum of £300; an employee guilty of an offence may be fined up to £75.

162 We have heard it suggested that these fines are sufficient and that the real penalty lies in being obliged to attend a criminal court. When we talked to people on the shop floor about the size of the fines, they said they thought it would hardly be noticed by a large firm. We think this is right. If justice is to be seen to be done, a sliding scale, according to the number of employees, would be more appropriate.

163 The 'psychological penalty' for a firm could also be increased by obliging the manager responsible for safety matters to attend the Court to answer the charge. This would not usually be the safety officer but the manager ultimately responsible and to whom the safety officer reports.

Conclusion

164 This study was not aimed at fundamental discovery about human behaviour but rather at the way in which what is already known can usefully be applied to the prevention of accidents in the workshop. We wanted to know the relative importance of the various factors causing accidents, and to suggest practical ways of reducing the accident rate.

165 A great deal is already known about accidents and human errors generally. It has been shown before that they increase with work load and outside an optimal range of temperature, and that they decrease with experience of the task. Much is known about how to design or modify machinery or work places, so that they are not hazardous; how to fit jobs to people and people to jobs and how to train them in safe methods of work.

166 In our workshops, we found that only a little of what is known had been applied. This seemed to be the result of a gap in communication between 'the office', where the knowledge could be obtained and the shop floor, where it needed application.* Our recommendations, therefore, emphasise the organisation of accident prevention work in a factory, in such a way that this gap is bridged.

167 The three factors we found to be of over-riding influence on the accidents in this study were:

(*a*) that risks were so much an integral part of work systems as at present

---

* i.e. knowledge both of techniques and of where to apply them. Incidentally to this research, we have found factory records bearing on accidents to be inaccurate; safety officers were found categorising inaccurate data in inappropriate ways and drawing meaningless conclusions therefrom. The essence of strictly objective injury recording is given at the Appendix para. 256 *et seq.*

arranged, that the more work was done, the more accidents occurred;

(b) that the risks which accompanied each task were specific and could be changed by changing details of the task;

(c) that people reduced their accident rate by gaining experience, i.e. they learned to avoid risks. But this experience was also highly specific and became blurred after time spent on other tasks.

168 It follows that the two main lines of a successful accident prevention policy must be a method of **design and layout,** which will eliminate hazards currently being built into systems of work, and **training,** to reduce the effects of inexperience.

169 Basically, the necessary change in design involves the way of thinking about work and the rightful functions of people vis-a-vis machines. It also involves a further spread of what we already know about accident prevention. Such changes are for the adult education system and will be fully effective only in the long term.

170 On the other hand, training can be introduced in a year or two and will be a patent attempt to tackle the problem at shop floor level. The importance of being seen to do something in the workshops cannot be over-emphasised. To make people more aware of risks and what can, and should, be done about them will result in a social pressure to really do more. This will add force to the change in design thinking which is the main solution to the problem.

171 Safety training can be a snag. A general social pressure to do something about risks might embarrass industrial management because it can see itself as the executive of the action required. If the management of a factory sets up a training programme which teaches people that certain of the systems in the factory involve risk of injury, it lays itself open to allegations that it is not doing enough to re-design the systems and eliminate the risks. This might be a root of the apathy we observed. In some cases, it may need strong governmental and public pressure to overcome it.

Recommendations

Multiple approach

172 This research has convinced us that tasks are highly specific; that the risks to which an individual worker may be subject are numerous and not always obvious to him; and that these risks can be changed by changing details of the work. Yet many people still think about accidents and tend to classify them and allocate blame as though they had single causes. A campaign is required to change this attitude. Several factors affect accidents and it follows that any one accident can usually be prevented in more than one way. The multiple approach needs emphasis.

173 There is an amusing example of this in the advertisements, for XXXX Ventilators, which have drawn attention to a relationship between temperature and accidents. We can endorse this to the extent that we have no doubt that comfortable working conditions are a pre-requisite for minimum accidents. But we found people coped with heat by reducing the work they did or by adjusting clothing. So long as they can do this, temperature is more important from the point of view of production than of accidents.

The parameters of safe system design

174 The first and most obvious need of industry is careful thought at the design stage about the way machines and people are to be combined in a system to do work. Many of the systems we have seen appeared to have been designed from the point of view of 'hardware engineering', forgetting the limitations of the human being. Thus, in mass production operations, people were expected to repeat complex actions with perfect consistency, time after time. And were expected to avoid danger by instant reaction to warning stimuli. When they failed at either of these activities, they laid themselves open to injury. Yet these are both activities at which people are known to be unreliable and slow; they are far better done by machine.

175 On the other hand, in jobs such as machine setting and maintenance or pushing a barrow, accidents occurred because the people involved failed to anticipate the danger and made faulty decisions about the appropriate action. Yet anticipation and decision-making are activities to which people are peculiarly suited, if they are trained in recognition of the warning signs and in the variety of possible actions.

176 In total, we are often expecting too much of people, giving them jobs which machines should do, and at the same time, neglecting to train and make full use of people in those activities at which human beings are far superior to machines.

The ergonomic approach . . .

177 The most hopeful approach to new thought about work is what the ergonomist calls 'systems design'. This first analyses the job to be done and then assigns the various activities between the people and the hardware, according to the special capabilities of each. Thus, the hardware is designed round the man, so that his role does not overtax his capabilities (and the ergonomist would follow his design by training the man, to enhance the abilities he will be using).

. . . needs teaching

178 Systems design needs teaching to engineers, designers and managers, as a logical framework around the vast accumulation of safety and training technology which exists already.

A diploma course for the professional

179 For the student who intends to specialise in advising others about systems design, safety technology and training techniques, there is a need for a series of courses leading to a diploma which will imply professional status. The courses for this must include general ergonomics, systems design, a review of present safety technology and law, tutoring in training techniques for achieving specific behavioural objectives, and applied psychology. This diploma would be for those with industrial experience (gained previously or simultaneously). We trust that the Department of Safety and Hygiene at Aston University will lead the way and that the subjects will thereby be helped to attain wide social emphasis.

Courses for students of other specialities

180 Two types of course are needed for students specialising in other disciplines: one session per week in the second year of a degree or diploma, to give the new blood of industry a grounding in this way of thinking. And for existing practitioners short courses which will give them an appreciation of systems design as a point of view for such part of safety and training technology as is appropriate to their own industry. The latter course will have to be 'customer-designed', to cover the appropriate technology.

Revision of syllabuses

181 We recommend universities and other Further Education Examination Boards to revise their syllabuses. This need not involve enlargement overall; we suggest a review of priorities. For example:

(a) The Council of Engineering Institutions' examination includes the subject of Mine Safety Engineering but there is nothing equivalent for the much larger proportion of engineers who will go into general industry, about which there is a more extensive safety technology. The Council demands a compulsory subject in the Part 2 examination, entitled 'The Engineer in Society'. This syllabus includes a study of historical aspects of industry and of 'Public relations and communications to learned societies'. How many engineers need this in preference to knowledge of how to keep their employees' fingers intact?

(b) The Department of Education and Science issued a Course Bulletin (No. 3) for Diplomas in Management. It says of Stage II that, 'the basic decision-making tools, such as statistical methods, costing methods and operational research techniques, are brought, so far as is practicable and relevant, into all parts of this course and *linked with the human aspects, problems of leadership and decision-implementation*'. Those last phrases could be interpreted by some college staffs as no more than the 'man management' that was taught to young officers in the Armed Services 20 years ago. It would be more meaningful to link the advanced techniques, described in the first part of the sentence, with – 'productive work, especially considered as the result of arranging men, machines and environment in a harmonious system'.

Attention by the Industrial Training Boards

182 We also recommend Industrial Training Boards to ensure that appreciation of the need for systems design and safety technology on the shop floor is part of all the appropriate short courses by which they are seeking to up-date the techniques of existing supervision and management.

The problem in the workshops ...

183 Some of the appreciation courses for management will reach shop supervision but apart from this, none of our recommendations so far will properly bridge the gap between shop floor and office. Yet it is on the shop floor that safety and training technology must be practised and it is there that we observed it to be sadly lacking. We felt sure that all the jobs we were watching could be taught on the shop floor and we know most of them were originally (and badly) taught there. So we now turn to the more specific problem of improving the workshops which already exist and will persist in unsatisfactory man-machine systems until the new design thinking which we advocate has become effective. Here lies the larger problem. We recommend a solution but with a reminder that in the absence of systems design, it is a partial solution.

... can be helped by training ...

184 An effective use of existing safety technology on the shop floor requires knowledgeable people in each workshop for most of the time. We think this is the only way in which innovations can be encouraged, followed through and maintained. The constant attendance is also necessary to bridge the communication gap between office and shop floor. At present, we do not think any office-based staff-member can be regarded as competent within the social organisation of the shop floor, because he is not sufficiently known and accepted there. But he can act as a link, if his duties provide a reason for frequent visits.

... with the co-operation of the Industrial Training Boards

185 Bearing in mind the current up-surge in training activities and the help which can be given to them by the Industrial Training Boards, we propose that a comprehensive system of shop floor trainers be the 'workshop end' of a firm's safety organisation and that their link to top management and up-to-date information be via an office-based but workshop-visiting supervisor.

Skills and knowledge required of the trainer

186 Shop floor trainers need teaching skills so that they can assist in the rapid allocation of recruits and shorten the inexperience effect. This they can obtain from a general course on how to train; such courses are already in existence. They also need safety knowledge but this need is too specific for a general course to be entirely satisfactory, although a brief one might be designed as a basis. The shop floor trainer needs to know about safety as it affects the shop in which he is going to work; there will be aspects quite unique in that shop.

Sources of safety knowledge

187   There are three sources of this knowledge. The first is a proper analysis of the injury records for that shop. These will give some clues to the more commonly occurring accidents; we deal with how to find these clues in the Appendix para. 256 *et seq.*

188   The second is knowledge about those risks which rarely cause injury but from which injury may be serious. Few, if any, of those risks will have materialised and caused injury in any one shop, so knowledge of these can be obtained only from country-wide knowledge of similar shops, such as has been gathered by the Factory Inspectorate, and some of the employers' associations and RoSPA.

189   The third is detailed knowledge of the tasks going on in the shop and this can be obtained only by working in that shop.

What each worker must be taught

190   Most shop floor operators work in a narrow field, in both the technological and geographical senses. The skill and knowledge required for each one's job is therefore limited. This applies to the accident pre-vention content of their training just as much as to the general content. For any one operator, safety training can usefully be considered in three parts:

(*a*)   safe conduct in the factory generally; e.g. how to avoid being run down by a fork-lift truck;

(*b*)   safe methods in the particular section of the workshop; e.g. avoidance of special hazards such as might be connected with a local machine;

(*c*)   safe methods in each of the tasks which the operator may perform; e.g. which type of package is dangerous to handle and how to avoid injury when obliged to handle it.

Where to find trainers

191   It follows that the most fruitful source of trainers for any one workshop will be the more intelligent people who are already experienced in that shop. These might be found amongst the setters or chargehands but such people are often indispensable in their present roles.* The bright young apprentice who makes himself expert at every job in the shop should be considered. The general need is for one or more of the more communicative, adaptable people to be specially trained.

192 Trainers could be introduced to a workshop from outside, if they were expert at training for the type of work going on and were prepared to study the local needs.

Supervision of trainers

193 Shop floor trainers need supervision, to guide them in their technique and keep them in touch with the latest knowledge. A training supervisor will act as the channel whereby the external safety knowledge mentioned at paras. 187/8 will be passed to the shop floor. He (or she) will need to spend much of his time on the shop floor, conferring, interalia, with his shop floor trainers. A training supervisor, obliged by his normal duties to be on the shop floor frequently, will inevitably talk to foremen, setters, chargehands and operators and can thereby influence them, as well as his own shop floor trainers. This, in our view, is the key to the closure of the 'communication gap'.

Training-and-safety officers

194 It follows from this that we do not see the role of safety officer as a separate entity at all; we see him (or her) as a part of the training function. In a factory of say 300 people, one and the same person might well be the training-and-safety officer, with perhaps only one training-and-safety supervisor and three trainers on his staff. In a factory of 3,000 people, there would be a director of training and safety, controlling several training-and-safety supervisors and many trainers. Such a group could well have a safety specialist amongst them who would see that each supervisor had knowledge appropriate to the sections of the factory for which he is responsible.

195 The training-and-safety officer will have an additional function in his 'office', as distinct from his 'shop floor' role. As part of management,

---

* The traditional role of the chargehand tends to diminish if work structuring (job enlargement) techniques are used to promote responsible working groups. The chargehand can then become a trainer.

he should be able to influence his colleagues in their appreciation of the limitations of human beings. His knowledge of what can and what cannot be expected of training will be useful in dissuading management that a man can be thought of as an extension of a machine.

196   We thus recommend a complete merger of safety with training. Their separate professional institutions should be encouraged to amalgamate, or at least to co-ordinate their activities.

N.B.

Insurance is not prevention

197   Some safety officers appear to spend time dealing with insurance claims. A firm line must be drawn between these activities and those of training-and-safety. The objectives of the two are disparate.

198   The insurance claims man is concerned with minimising his payments out. He wants to blame the injured party for any loss. He wants reports and statements from witnesses, on either of which legal arguments about blame can be based. The idea of blame inhibits constructive thought about accident prevention, especially if the blame is imagined to rest on the (absent) injured party.

199   On the other hand, the training-and-safety man is concerned with minimising injuries. Whilst no one would quarrel with him if he wanted to know exactly how an accident happened in his factory, his concern must be for the changes in design, layout, working arrangements and training, which will reduce or eliminate injury. This is a strictly objective activity, and it needs to be seen as such if all concerned are to co-operate willingly.

200   Most firms have someone who specialises in insurance; this person should handle all claims under employers' liability and national insurance.*

Expansion of the Factory Inspectorate

201   We would like to see the Factory Inspectorate increase its staff in an effort to spread its expert knowledge. Although the Inspectorate (and other bodies) issue booklets of safety technology, these do not reach the shop floor. An enlarged Inspectorate would be able to extend its role to

---

* If reports to the Factory Inspectorate continue to be used by the lawyers in preparing a case for the Courts, then writing these reports also falls into the province of the insurance man, in our opinion.

include teaching and to maintain more frequent contact with training-and-safety officers. Additionally, frequent visits by a factory inspector could do much to convince management generally that safety is important and that government cares about it. All factory inspectors will, of course, need to be sufficiently familiar with training technology to be able to talk to trainers on their own terms. They will also need knowledge of systems design. A diploma of the type envisaged in para. 179 would be appropriate to the future factory inspector.

First-aid records

202 Analysis of a factory's first-aid records by area and then by agent of injury, is a useful tool for the safety organisation in that factory. The need to keep first-aid records from which this can be done must be publicised and taught. We would like to see the contents of our Appendix 6 (para. 256 *et seq.*) included in the Safety Health and Welfare booklet on 'First-aid in Factories' and in the syllabus of the Institution of Industrial Safety Officers.

National Statistics

203 If our experience is typical, officially reported figures for three-day lost-time accidents are still much smaller than the truth. Yet many of the victims of these 'lost' injuries must be receiving treatment under the National Health Service, and a doctor is supplying a First Certificate. If this certificate could always show (by a tick in a 'box') whether or not the patient apparently sustained the injury at work, the Department of Health and Social Security could compare their figures with those of the Factory Inspectorate, to get a better picture. However, it must be remembered that it is a picture distorted by the different clerical arrangements of different firms, the wish to avoid blame, ignorance of procedure and differences in the compensation available from national and local sources.

Social Security

204 Equalisation of national insurance compensation for sickness and for work injury is also needed as a matter of social justice. It would benefit accident prevention because it would help to foster the opinion which regards accidents as a disease. And, like disease, something controllable by specific preventive measures. It would benefit accident reporting by removing a source of bias. (The sick-pay schemes run by some firms are a source of bias, acting in the opposite direction to that of the present industrial injury benefit.)

Legislation

205 The legislation we would like to see is that which will encourage firms (and unions) to re-design machines, layout and systems generally, and to train. For example, it would help if Section 29 of the Factories Act 1961, which requires an employer to provide a safe place of work, also required him to maintain a safe system of work.*

206 As a country, we seem desperately short of people with an awareness of how to tackle system design and training, with human limitations and injury prevention in mind. Licensing of factory managers and training-and-safety officers would help, if the granting of a licence was conditional upon satisfactory completion of approved professional training (as in paras. 179/180).

207 The true cost of injuring people is hardly noticed by an industrial firm in its accounts (see para. 69 *et seq.*). It would help if it was. We suggest an industrial levy, sufficient to pay compensation to people unable to work because of injuries, and to finance the accident work of the National Health Service and the Factory Inspectorate. (Schemes roughly along these lines exist in Canada but do not, so far as we know, finance part of the medical service.)

Union Information Services

208 What little we saw of union activity, aimed at informing their members about procedures for making a civil claim for damages for personal injury, was ineffective (see para. 160). The information was not reaching where it was needed, and some of it was given in an indigestible form. It would appear that the union organisation also has its 'communication gap'. This is hardly surprising, in the light of the even greater geographical separation of shop floor and union district office. We recommend unions to improve their information services.

209 The Employed Person (Health and Safety) Bill, talked about in 1970, proposed that safety representatives should be appointed from amongst established workers. Although, as drafted, the Bill gave them incongruent aims (see Appendix para. 700 *et seq.*) the advantages of having some workers made specially aware of accident prevention techniques is obvious. We suggest unions will need to train each safety representative in accident prevention appropriate to the workshop he is in.

* 'System' has a narrower meaning for a lawyer than for an ergonomist. If we explain that the lawyer's 'system' plus his 'place of work' is roughly equivalent to the ergonomist's 'system', we trust our ergonomist readers will forgive us.

Appendices

NOTE ON STATISTICAL SIGNIFICANCE

210 Probability is the likelihood of a relationship occurring purely by chance. This can be expressed in different ways; for example, a probability level of five per cent means that the result could occur by chance five times in one hundred. A probability level expressed as $p < \cdot 01$ means that the likelihood of the result occurring by chance is less than one in one hundred.

211 In this report we have quoted as statistically significant those results whose likelihood of occurring by chance was no more than five per cent. We have also mentioned results which might have occurred by chance between five and ten times in one hundred; they suggest trends that might deserve further investigation.

JEAN MARTIN

Appendix 1
Aims of the research

212 The original research plan proposed an investigation on the shop floor, along interdisciplinary lines. Methods were to be developed to study the interaction and combined effects of environment and personal factors contributing to accidents. There were three immediate aims:

(*a*) to improve systems of investigation and recording to meet the practical needs of accident prevention;

(*b*) to improve the identification and control of the factors which have to be taken into account in constructing field experiments for testing hypotheses and the effects of remedies;

(*c*) to seek such recognisable classes among the events and personal characteristics associated with accidents as may afford a basis for prediction.

213 In its long term, the research was to be an attempt to bridge the gap between studies emanating from the laboratory on the one hand and practice, that of accident prevention, on the other. It sought to re-appraise 'hypotheses in terms of the observations which can normally be made in the practical situation and to develop techniques of investigation and experiment in the field'. In simpler terms, it aimed to help the practical man as well as the research worker in learning what to look for in accident prevention and how to look.

214 The research plan entailed the presence of observers in four departments of factories where the work and its conditions were well contrasted. The observers were to compile detailed records of the work and its environment, and records about all employees in the departments, under the following heads.

(*a*) **Description of the work and environment** in the selected departments: (i) the operations carried out, rest pauses, rhythm and pace of working, interruptions; (ii) the arrangement of the work, display, controls, posture; (iii) the physical environment, temperature, humidity, air velocities, visibility, toxic substances and other sources of adverse physical conditions; (iv) rates and methods of payment, types and nature of incentives; (v) management, type and quality of supervision; (vi) training; (vii) selection by management or resulting from the nature of the work or other causes;

(viii) any special characteristics of the work and its environment revealed during the investigation.

(*b*) **Personal records of employees:** (i) age, sex, dependants; (ii) address, home circumstances, source of additional responsibility or stress; (iii) length of employment, previous employments; (iv) work record, lateness, absence; (v) any medical information which can be made available.

215 With this information as background, *studies were to be made of every untoward incident resulting in an injury to a workman, and to damage to machinery or products or clothing* where these were associated with human error.* Each would be matched by studies of two people ('controls') in the same department, chosen so as to eliminate some factors which need to be considered. Thus one of the controls was to be the occupant of the workplace next to the victim, in the hope that this would take some account of environmental conditions. The other control was to be someone 'of the same sex in the same occupation and of similar age, experience and responsibility who has not sustained an accident within the specified period'. This was an attempt to match out some of the personal characteristics. In the event, both these controls had to be modified for reasons of practicability, which we deal with in the body of this report.

216 This use of controls was aimed at reducing the size of the sample population required to obtain statistically valid conclusions from information which was bound to have a large number of variables. A small sample size was required in each department so that the observer could know all individuals and collect detailed information from each.

217 Since there can be no guarantee that any research plan will achieve its full aims, its value needed to be assessed in other ways. No previous attempt has yet been made to observe a working situation systematically and continuously over a long period of time and there could be little doubt that this alone would help to identify factors contributing to accidents in terms of observations which can actually be made in factories. Secondly, concepts derived from more theoretical studies could be re-examined in these terms; theories about the behaviour of groups, for example, could at least be put to the test of seeing the ways in which group behaviour could be observed in practice. Again, accident statistics are notoriously affected by quite small changes in things which influence reporting and a close study could be made of the factors that influence people's readiness to report their injuries and of the accuracy of reporting by people responsible for keeping records.† Some preliminary study could be made of the relation between

---

* There were too few 'damage only' incidents to make an analysis worthwhile. In small work, damage often passes un-noticed until the inspection stage.

† For example one company had four different crews of workers employed on different shifts, each having its own first-aid room attendant, who was instructed to record every patient treated in the first-aid room. A study to try to discover the reason for different accident rates in these four crews showed it to lie in the attendant's differing interpretation of the instruction.

minor and major accidents and of the characteristics of accident repeaters.

218 It was proposed that, at some final stage, formal interviewing and testing of a selected sample of the workshop population could be used to supplement information not obtained in the ordinary course of the study.

219 The original proposal allowed some six months for the appointment and training of staff, compiling basic records and trials of recording methods in the factories. The next two years were to be devoted to the accident reporting, observation, interviewing, maintenance and checking of basic records, preliminary analyses and formal interviews and tests. The final 18 months were to be concerned with final checking of data, completion of analyses and final reporting. Many things, which appear in this report, have interfered with this time-table but we do not think the validity of our conclusions is significantly affected.

CAROLINE WARNE
P. I. POWELL

Appendix 2
Difficulties of data collection

220 We found that the collection of information about each individual's work and accidents, accurately related to time and circumstances, was very time consuming. Factory records were of limited help only, because they were mainly directed either towards overall input/output finance over long periods, such as a month or a quarter, or towards paying employees weekly. Thus a strictly accurate figure for the output of an individual or a shop for a day, or even for a week, was often unobtainable because few bothered with such precise demarcation of time.

221 In shops where a bonus system was operating, records existed showing the tasks done in some detail, but we found that times recorded were often inaccurate, and work was carried over to the next day or week when in fact it had been finished, or vice versa. For wages purposes, this does not matter; what is left off the record for today will go in tomorrow and no one minds. But it was insufficient for our research.

222 Attendance records can also be time consuming to collect. The original records (clock-cards or a book) are usually accurate, but where a firm transfers the information to an absence record, errors can creep in.

223 So far as the accidents were concerned, the original research proposal suggested that the foreman or a similar class of person in authority in the factory would be able to collect details of accidents for us as each occurred, but we found that this was not possible for several reasons. These were:

(*a*) The foreman was not always there.

(*b*) He is not known by the rest of the shop as a person specially interested in accidents, and therefore he did not hear of accidents other than those he sent for treatment at the surgery or first-aid. At two shops we did try to persuade all foremen to tell us when an accident occurred on their section and the response varied from 100 per cent of those sent to the first-aid, to none.

(*c*) The information required was complex. Foremen did not have the time to collect it, and did not appreciate some of the things we need to look at.

(*d*) We thought we would miss some enlightening comments about supervision.

(*e*) People bias reports to conceal anything which they think reflects un-favourably on them (or on associates they care about).

(*f*) Different people report differently and we could therefore expect different emphases of reporting from each foreman. This would introduce a bias which we could not eliminate in analysis.

So we have collected this information ourselves.

P. I. POWELL

Appendix 3
Statistical Controls

224 To obtain satisfactory controls in the typical factory situation is difficult, because people doing apparently similar work do in fact perform tasks which are sufficiently different in detail that the risks of injury are dissimilar. The following paragraphs refer mainly to developments in method whilst we were observing the machine and assembly shops. Broadly similar methods were used subsequently in the despatch department and the rolling mill.

Controls
225 The controls were two people chosen to be like the accident victim in certain defined ways. Gathering the information pertinent to the time of the accident from controls as well as from an accident victim helped in two ways:

(*a*) it enabled us to eliminate the effect of certain chosen variables from the analysis, thus simplifying the method of analysis;

(*b*) it added to our fund of information about the sample because it prevented us from restricting our contacts to accident victims at any time.

226 The research proposal suggested that the first control should be the person who occupied the work place nearest to the accident victim, the implication being that this person would be in the same environment. But temperature and humidity varied insignificantly from place to place in our shops, whereas many aspects of the work itself varied from person to person even on superficially similar machines. Therefore we altered the first control to a task control. Ideally, this would be someone doing the identical thing to the identical component, so that in any analysis it would be possible to eliminate the effects of the task and, of course, of the macro-environment and see what other factors affected the accident. In practice, because the identical task occurred rarely, we decided on three criteria, by which a first control could be selected with reasonable convenience.

227 The criteria we decided to adopt were certain broad categories of task*, machine and component, in that order of priority. We found we had just over

---

* In this context the 'task' was one selected from a limited list referred to in the next sentence. Examples are drilling, tapping, cleaning, oiling, packing.

130 categories of task which might be done in the two shops and these the observers had to be able to recognise on sight. The machines were grouped according to conventional type, e.g., capstan lathes, vertical drill, with one or two special sub-divisions where we could see obvious different classes of risk, e.g., power presses fed with either the individual component pieces or by a continuous strip of metal. Components were compared by shape, size and material. Usually it was possible to find a first control where the risks inherent in the job were generally comparable, and the observer was then expected to make notes on the comparison. Sometimes it was impossible to find a first control who was at all appropriate.

228 For the second control the proposal called for an employee of 'the same sex in the same occupation and of similar age, experience and responsibility, who has not sustained an accident within the specified period'. The proposal did not say what the 'specified period' should be but, after examining factory accident records for our population we thought six months would be workable. In practice, we found that more people had accidents than were recorded and the possible second controls dwindled to so small a number that it would not have been statistically meaningful. Consequently, we decided to have criteria which would provide a more constant and simple way of selecting the second control. So we restricted our criteria to sex, experience (expressed as length of service with the company) and age, in that order of priority. We found this gave us a reasonable choice of second controls for almost everyone in the shops, when we used limits of plus or minus 10 per cent on age and plus or minus 25 per cent on experience. We ignored 'responsibility' because we could not cope with four criteria in the practical situation.

229 We maintained an index, showing the age and experience of each person, together with the names of the four people who most nearly satisfied the criteria; this gave a reasonable choice and was capable of entry on one line of an index book. There were a few cases where four people were not available and we then chose at least two who most nearly fitted the criteria. We used each chosen second control in rotation, and so gathered information widely in the population.

CAROLINE WARNE
P. I. POWELL

Appendix 4
First-aid records - comparisons with our observations and some factors affecting them

Treatment of injuries

230   The work injuries we observed in the machine and assembly shops were treated as shown in the following table:

Table 2 – Medical treatment of people in machine and assembly shops

Treatment	Machine men	Machine women	Assembly men	Assembly women
Hospital*	36	10	5	23
Works surgery*	300	117	73	368
Self-treated	61	60	9	137
Not treated	131	92	19	173
Unknown	11	5	3	15

* The treatments marked with an asterisk indicate injuries which were recorded by the works.

Proportion of injuries recorded in two shops

231   Whether or not an injured party sought treatment at the works surgery must, of course, have depended to a considerable extent on the nature and severity of the injury, and these, in turn, reflect the nature of the work which the injured party was doing. Hence we find geographical and sex differences affecting the proportion of injuries recorded, as shown in the table below.

Table 3 – Proportion of observed injuries recorded by men and by women

	Machine men	Machine women	Assembly men	Assembly women
Total injuries observed	539	284	109	716
Recorded at works surgery	336	127	78	391
	(62%)	(45%)	(72%)	(55%)

Distance to the works surgery

232   A possible factor influencing the propensity to seek treatment at a works surgery is the distance one has to walk to reach it. We thought that people who worked near to the surgery might go there for dressings more readily than those

who had further to go. We could not study this in the machine shop because different sections had widely differing accident rates (see Appendix para. 282), and because the sections were not widely different in their distance from the surgery. We studied the relationship between the distance of the assembly lines from the surgery and the accident rate for the lines, but did not obtain a significant result. However, there are other factors which would have affected the result, such as the level of experience on the different lines, which we could not control for.

Variations in recording in one shop

233   In the machine shop no-one was more than 120 yards from the surgery, yet we still found marked differences in the proportion of injuries recorded, as the following table shows:

Table 4 – Proportion of observed injuries recorded at the surgery

	Men	Women
Lathes	63%	54%
Power presses	61%	41%
Grinders	64%	62%
Drills	46%	36%
Milling machines	62%	22%
Gear cutters	60% app. *	30% app. *

* Very small numbers

234   The tendency for women to be allocated to lighter work with less risk of serious injury is generally reflected in the figures. This explains, in particular, the low recording for women milling machine operators. Most of them operated burnishing machines and the typical injury was a very occasional splinter. The women on this section carried their own Elastoplast. Another low record occurred for women operating drills. The reason here was not so much the triviality of the injuries, although many of these were splinters and small cuts, but the poor opinion of the surgery treatment held by several of the operators. Surgery treatment for injured fingers had sometimes been a covering with open-weave material, which tended to catch on the drills and was a source of further, more serious, risk. The men in this section were also low recorders compared with the men in the remaining sections of the shop and we think the reason was the same.

Effect of recruitment on injury recording

235   We calculated Spearman's Rank Correlation Co-efficients between recruitment and total recorded and non-recorded accidents. The results are shown in the table following.

236   These figures show that there is a closer relationship between recruitment and non-reported accidents than between recruitment and reported accidents. This indicates that new recruits do not report as high a proportion of their

accidents as people who have been there longer.

Table 5 – Correlations between recruitment* and injuries

Recruitment and :	Rank Correlation	Significance level
Total injuries	0·53	1%
Recorded injuries	0·43	5%
Non-recorded injuries	0·55	1%

* 'recruitment' here means the number of people recruited per month.

Difference between recorded and total observed injuries over the days of the week
237 The following table shows the distribution over the days of the week for injuries recorded by the surgery and the total observed by us.

Table 6 – Recorded and observed injuries

	Mon	Tues	Wed	Thur	Fri
Recorded	169	176	198	207	153
Total observed	297	316	360	306	253
Therefore not recorded	128	140	162	99	100

238 It can be seen that these do not show quite the same pattern, there being most non-recorded and total injuries on Wednesdays, but most recorded injuries on Thursdays. This may be due to Thursday being pay day and a day when people do not work so hard and so feel they can spare the time to go to the medical centre.

Recollection of accident time
239 We looked at the distribution of accident times in ten-minute intervals and found that there were peaks in the distribution when the ten-minute period included the hour or half-hour and, to a lesser extent, the quarter-hour. This is attributed to a tendency for people to approximate to the nearest hour or half-hour if they are unsure of the time of the accident, and is of course commonly observed in other situations.

Time lapse in observing accidents
240 Much of the time people who had accidents told us about them soon after the accident, or someone else told us when an accident had occurred. However, there was occasionally a gap of several days before we heard about an accident, and we know we missed some altogether. We thought that any appreciable time lapse would result in a loss of information about the accident. We attempted to study this by comparing the information obtained about accidents which were recorded within an hour of their occurrence, with those where there was a lapse of at least three days. The descriptions of the accidents were classified as little, intermediate or full, for samples of the two groups of accidents. We found no significant difference between the groups with respect to how detailed was the description, but we found that there were differences between the various observers. Some observers could express themselves in fewer words than others.

JEAN MARTIN

Appendix 5
Factors influencing the accident records at a shop without a fully staffed surgery

241 There are two ways in which the recording of accidents can take place:

(*a*) the recording of the injury in the first-aid or surgery records;

(*b*) the reporting of the accident on National Insurance Form BI.76, Department of Employment form 43, or some equivalent provided by the employer.

242 The former should take place on the occasion of any injury that is treated at the first-aid facilities. The latter should take place whenever an accident causes three or more days lost time, is a 'dangerous occurrence' (as statutorily defined), and, in the case of a form provided by the employer, whenever an accident victim desires to report his injury, even if this is not required by law.

243 At our shop without a fully staffed surgery, less than 5 per cent of the accidents we discovered were recorded *at all*. Recording under (*a*) first-aid records was just non-existent. The only accidents for which the shop had records were those reported under (*b*) on a form provided by the employer.

244 There was not a proper surgery or nurse at this shop, the first-aid being organised and carried out by members of the staff, trained by the St John Ambulance Brigade. There was a small first-aid room, which contained the barest essentials for treatment. The trained first-aiders did not consider it part of their function to record details of the treatments. A small notebook hung in the first-aid room, but the last entry in it referred to a member of the clerical staff having two aspirins two years before. Treatment was also available in an office where there was a small first-aid box, but no notebook. Over 50 men received treatment by the first-aiders during our period of observation.

245 The first-aiders were not encouraged to keep records. We found them most helpful at telling us verbally who they had treated, and this enabled us to discover accidents we may otherwise have missed. We did suggest to the first-aider who looked after the first-aid room that he noted basic details of treatment, but his attitude was that no-one would look at them. Given a greater awareness of the absolute necessity of having accurate records of the injuries that occur as an aid to their future prevention, we feel sure that the first-aiders would have been prepared to note details along the lines proposed in Appendix 6 (para. 256 *et seq.*).

246 To report an accident involved the victim in completing an accident form and citing one or more witnesses to the incident for corroboration of the description of the accident.

247 One member of the personnel department had a job which included the collection of reported accidents. Theoretically he handed out the accident form and, if necessary, helped the victim to complete it. He collected the relevant information from witnesses in writing. Practically, however, he was out of contact with the men, and it was the victim's job to go to the personnel department and ask for the accident form.

248 This appeared to be where the breakdown occurred. Victims of both minor and major accidents would sometimes go out of their way to tell us about their accidents and would also often tell the time clerks with whom they had personal contact when checking in and out, etc. The time clerks were very friendly with the majority of the men and in fact fulfilled some of the functions of the personnel department. Men were prepared to ask them about problems, yet it sometimes needed considerable persuasion by the time clerks to get a man to go to the personnel department.

249 The difficulty lay in the fact that the personnel department appeared as a separate entity to most of the men. This was partly because some of the men did not appreciate the attitudes and work of some of the personnel people. On the other hand, one of the time clerks was a man who was popular and always willing to be of assistance with problems, both inside and outside his defined job.

250 Most of the men said, when asked why they had not bothered to report accidents, that there was no point in doing so. The only accidents which were reported were four where the injury was potentially serious enough to cause a possible future absence, and 11 which did cause absence. There were 18 other accidents, resulting in some absence, which were not reported and many more, difficult to estimate, which could have caused possible future absence, e.g., minor strains and untreated cuts, etc. The four reported accidents which did not cause absence, were all reported on the victim's initiative, the victim in two cases being a supervisor. Four of the 11 which caused absence were reported because of the direct encouragement of a supervisor, three because of the influence of a time clerk, and the remaining four on the initiative of the victims.

251 An efficient system is one which allows men to report their accidents without wasting time, which may incur the displeasure of their workmates and supervisors, and without fear of being a marked man. The latter reason was mentioned by many of the men, who saw accident reporting more as a safeguard for the company in the event of a claim than as an aid to accident prevention. There was an in-built suspicion of forms, the purpose of which was not fully understood.* If the reasons for reporting accidents were explained clearly to the men, the reaction might have been very different. We found during our year

---

* Could it be that they did understand it, and were quite rightly suspicious? – P.I.P.

of study that the majority of men became freer and more communicative about their accidents as they accepted and understood our role.

252 The doctor's First Certificate, which is required in cases of absence, notes the reason for absence, and is often a pointer to an industrial accident that would otherwise go unheeded. The certificate was dealt with by a clerk who had no responsibility in the field of accidents; the victim was simply noted as being 'sick', and no enquiries were made about the accident after his return to work. This was true of all cases except those of long absence where the man had to undergo a company medical examination before returning to work. An accident form was normally completed in such cases. Several cases arose of men being registered as sick instead of injured.

253 Probably the easiest practical way of improving accident reporting within the present system would be to leave it to the time clerks to give out the accident forms and collect them when they are completed. The personnel department, although not far from the men physically, was too remote psychologically. The time clerks already recorded reasons for absence and collected such doctors' certificates as are handed in, so this extra duty would not seem out of context.

254 Given a convenient system of reporting (and one which did not appear to be collecting evidence for a defence in the case of a legal claim for damages – P.I.P.), we see no reason why most of the 72 accidents resulting in moderate or severe injury which we knew about should not have been reported properly. As it was, 57 of them escaped 'official' notice.

255 Summing up, there was at this shop an incentive *not* to report any but the most serious accidents. The factors which contributed were primarily loss of time, suspicion, acceptance of minor injuries, and the reporting procedure itself. We recommend that:

(*a*) Someone in easy communication with shop floor personnel should deal with reported accidents; at our shop the best man seemed to be one of the time clerks.

(*b*) First-aiders should be encouraged to record details of treatments.

(*c*) These records should be regularly analysed by a member of staff responsible for safety.

(*d*) Supervisors should encourage the recording of accidents.

(*e*) The men themselves should be informed of the possible advantage to them of accurate accident records.

(*f*) A requirement to produce names of witnesses should be dropped.

(*g*) Something should be seen to be done about accidents.   M. SIMON

Appendix 6
Surgery day-sheets
- a suggested minimum standard

256 Records of injuries at a factory surgery or first-aid post are usually kept by the medical or first-aid staff. Consequently they usually contain brief, accurate descriptions of the injuries, together with the name of the injured person and often the date and the time of treatment.

257 Many people lose sight of the fact that such records can be a valuable management tool, from which information can be obtained about what is going on inside the factory. Where injuries are occurring, time is being wasted and production lost. If this is occurring repeatedly, an overhaul of the system of work may well be justified, in an effort to reduce the loss.

258 If surgery records are to be used as a management tool, it is clear that the records must carry more information. The puzzle is to decide what information; how little can we get away with and still have a useful record? Surgery staff may be very busy, so brevity is the essential.

What information does management need?
259 The reduction or elimination of injury is a matter for management, but it needs to be told *what* is happening, *where* it is going on, and *how often*. All these may be gleaned from very simple entries in a surgery day-sheet.

What is happening?
260 The nature of the injury and the part of the body injured is required, and surgery records usually provide this amply. Records at first-aid boxes are not always so helpful and it is as a reminder to the amateur first-aider that we suggest the record should have separate headings for 'injury' and 'part of body'.

261 The 'agent of injury' is also required. The first-aider should ask 'What actually hit/cut you?' and elicit a concise answer.

Where is it happening?
262 Records often go astray here. The tendency is to record the name of the injured party and his 'department', but this can be interpreted in at least two ways. The department to which the man is attached for payment purposes may be the 'maintenance department', but he can be injured whilst working in the 'assembly department' or a variety of others. If management is to know where

injuries are happening, the record must be defined as 'place where accident occurred'. Here should be entered the name of the workshop and, if it is a large one, the part or section of it.

263 Hence a day-sheet in the form shown at Table 7. It shows management just where to go to look, if any enquiry into the circumstances of the injury is required.

Why not enter 'cause'?
264 Accidents are usually multi-causal. To try to assess some or any of these causes without a full enquiry and inspection of the scene will lead only to some superficial and subjective judgment, based on hearsay. Such judgments are a waste of the time of the surgery staff. If analyses of accidents are based on such flimsily-assessed, single causes, the resulting paperwork is worthless. It can be grossly misleading as a guide-line for action.

How often?
265 In factories or large workshops having a variety of work, it is sometimes an advantage to divide the injury records by workshop or section. How often this is done depends on the total number of injuries and the convenience of all concerned. If it is done daily, it is a very small task. The advantage of such division is that injury patterns peculiar to workshops or sections are thrown into relief. For example, six eye injuries amongst 173 total injuries can be overlooked but if a sub-division of the record shows five of them originating in one workshop, it shows a need for action.

266 It is also worthwhile looking for recurring agents of injury in one area. For example, if it is found that swarf accounts for a large number of injuries on, say, the lathes, it is worth trying to suppress its effects. If the injuries are mostly to the eyes, chip deflectors and spectacles might help. If the injuries are mostly to the hands and legs, is this the result of long swarf from stainless steel? Swarf breakers may help. The safety officer can go to the lathe section with some ideas already forming; no doubt he will have to elaborate or modify them when he sees what really is going on but he has made a start. (He should also read Appendix 29.)

P. I. POWELL

Table 7 – Typical first-aid day-sheet

SURGERY: DATE: DAY OF WEEK:

Time of accdt.	Name	Clock No.	Injury	Part of body	Place where it happened	Agent of injury	Treatment	Disposal
	John Smith		deep cut	ankle	lathes, m/c shop	swarf	clean and dress	hospital
	P. Brown		cut	1 FRH	drills, m/c shop	component	"	R.T.W.
	M. Green		FB	LE	yard	probably sand	irrigate	R.T.W.

The above abbreviations are commonly used. They mean:
FB   – foreign body
1FRH – first finger of right hand
LE   – left eye
m/c   – machine
RTW   – returned to work.

Appendix 7
A first look at some agents of injury

267 These paragraphs and tables were an attempt to see what were the most frequent causes of the injuries in the first 300 accidents in three sections of our machine shop.* The figures were compiled from our own records, which described the 'agent' of the injury – that is, the thing which cut or bruised or broke the bone of the victim. As you will see, we have classified these agents into six broad groups:

    Swarf
    Materials and components
    Machines and tools
    Bins, boxes and crates
    Passageways
    Other.

268 Two factors emerge at once. First, the numbers of accidents per section are grossly different. This is partly, but only partly, accounted for by the different number of operatives per section. Thus, the 'quantity' of risk differs from one section to another in the workshop. Secondly, the proportion of injuries resulting from the various groups of agents is different. Thus, the risks in one sort of machine work are different from those in another.

269 It is but a short step from this analysis to having a look at the work to which it applies and seeing for oneself how these agents of injury might be made less harmful.

270 Three risks which can result in serious disablement in lathe work are that of contact and entanglement with moving parts; dermatitis; and eye injury from flying swarf. We have had no serious disablement from any of these in the first 109 accidents in the lathe sections. There were some later on.

271 Such contact with moving parts as we have recorded has resulted in only minor cuts and scratches, perhaps fortuitously. In any lathe section, entanglement is a rare event and we have not experienced it at our site. Ties and scarves are not worn and most people work with sleeves no lower than the elbow. To take

* This preliminary analysis is not fully representative of the picture over the total period of observation but we think it sufficient to make the points clear.

Table 8 – Agents of injury in the lathe section

Agent of injury	Small lathes	Large lathes	Total	per cent
SWARF				
Direct cuts and burns from swarf	4	5	9	
Cuts from inclusions in cloths used for cleaning	2	0	2	39%
Foreign body in the eye	12	11	23	
Splinters	5	4	9	
MATERIAL AND COMPONENT				
Cuts from handling component when stationary	1	7	8	
Cuts from handling component when moving	4	3	7	15%
Abrasion from repeated handling of component	0	1	1	
MACHINE AND TOOLS				
Cut from outer ring of collet	0	1	1	
Nail torn by collet	1	3	4	
Cut by guard of collet	1	1	2	
Unguarded nips (1 was between tool in turret, as it came forward, and the collet)	2	0	2	33%
Stiff controls (blisters, abrasion, swelling)	2	2	4	
Cuts by turret tools, or holders or screws	6	8	14	
Cuts by cross slide tools	2	3	5	
Cuts by handling tools (including scrapes)	0	4	4	
BOXES				
Legs bruised by stacking near lathe	6	0	6	6%
Hand cut by stacking near lathe	1	0	1	
PASSAGEWAY				
Falls in	0	2	2	4%
Cuts from things in or near	1	1	2	
OTHER	1	2	3	3%
TOTAL	51	58	109	100%

an observation at random, on one occasion 10 operators out of 14 were working with their sleeves up. The reasons they gave for this fell into the following groups:

(*a*) the usual temperature of 19°C–22°C encourages it;

(*b*) the women prefer to work with bare fore-arms because they find it more comfortable and because it saves sleeves getting oily;

(*c*) some of the men have sleeveless overalls and shirts;

(*d*) the nylon overalls available to the women through the factory are all short-sleeved.

Whatever the reason, the effect is to avoid entanglement, although no operator mentions it.

272 Dermatitis has affected one operator in the past and this person is now restricted to dry jobs. No-one on the lathe sections has succumbed to dermatitis since we started recording. There is a medical screening of new recruits, which may be helping to reduce dermatitis.

273 Swarf accounts for 39 per cent of the injuries in the table and many of these are eye injuries. One has only to see the specks of metal adhering to an operator's face and hair to realise how high is the risk associated with flying swarf. We think we have probably started a reduction in the rate at which these injuries occur, because we happened to mention to the safety officer that the natural reaction of anyone getting something in the eye is to ask his mate to see if he can get it out. If he is successful, the injury is unlikely to be reported to the medical centre. The safety department is now issuing safety spectacles and encouraging their use, with a view to making the wearing of spectacles a condition of employment eventually. We mentioned our views about the need for comfort and fashionable appearance of safety spectacles (see Appendix 29, para. 646 *et seq.*) and this has resulted in the issue of some quite pleasant looking glasses, which most people seem to like. Even so, we notice that the operators do not wear them unless they appreciate that the job contains an eye risk.

274 There are two classifications in the table where the difference in the numbers for normal capstan and miniature capstan are surprisingly dissimilar. One of these is the cuts caused by handling a stationary component, from which the normal capstan operators suffer far more than the miniature capstan operators. This arises because the components dealt with on normal capstans are larger and, in general, have more sharp edges. The other classification is of bruises to the leg by boxes stacked near the lathe. These appear to occur exclusively on the miniature capstan section, where the operators are all women, sitting down to their work. They bruise their legs when swinging round and getting up from their chairs. It would be possible to stack boxes of components further away from the working position but then they would be out of reach of anyone sitting on the chair. On the normal machines, the operators are men and they all stand up to their work, because the lathes are larger and the reach required for the controls is longer. We recollect the ergonomic joke about the typical capstan lathe being 'designed for a man 4 ft high, with arms 3 ft long'. It seems to have more than a grain of truth.

275 The obvious risk of serious accident with a press is that of getting the hand nipped between the tools when the press operates. In our press shop, interlocked guards or fixed guards are widely used and this no doubt contributes to the

Table 9 – Agents of injury in the press section

Agent of injury	No.	per cent
SWARF		
Splinters – source unknown	2	
Splinters – wood, pallet	1	4%
Splinters – metal off component or material	3	
Splinters – inclusions in cloths used for cleaning	1	
MATERIAL AND COMPONENT		
Abrasions from repeated handling	4	
Cuts from handling component (mostly sheet metal)	63	
Cuts from new strip metal	30	
Cuts from scrap strip metal	22	72%
Cuts from other small scrap	7	
Cuts on steel banding	1	
Metal coil falling over onto foot	1	
MACHINES AND TOOLS		
Abrasions by repeated contact with tool	1	
Strain (setting heavy tools)	1	
Crush when tool slipped (setter)	1	
Cut on edge of machine or tools	16	
Cut and bruise by guard as it power closed	2	14%
Cut and bruise by guard as it fell on setter	1	
Crush between tools (setter)	1	
Uncovenanted release of spring loaded tools	2	
Cut on hand tools	1	
CONTROLS		
Bruise and cumulative abrasion	2	1%
METAL BOXES AND WIRE CRATES		
Tripped over box/crate	1	
Cut on box/crate	7	6%
Strains and sprains when moving box/crate	2	
Bruised on box/crate	1	
PASSAGEWAY		
Fall in	1	2%
Collision with doors and truck	2	
OTHER		
Oil splash in eye	1	1%
Nail projecting from bench	1	
TOTAL	179	100%

result that no operator succumbed to this risk. One setter nearly crushed his hand – a narrow escape from disaster – when inching a power press, with which he was unfamiliar. The guard interlocks have since been altered to eliminate this risk, even for setters.

276 The more serious accidents of those we have recorded so far in the press section have been the result of manoeuvring heavy press tools and the un-covenanted release of a large spring-loaded tool. All these accidents happened to setters of long experience with the firm, but performing a task which they had not done recently, if ever.

277 By far the largest proportion of injuries in the press shop are caused by the handling of thin sheet metal having sharp edges. Over 70 per cent of press shop injuries are caused in this way, compared with a mere 15 per cent in the lathe sections. As might be expected, the machines and tools cause a minor proportion of the injuries (14 per cent) but even so, two-thirds of these were cuts on sharp edges, which are needless on the parts of a press and its tools where operators have to put their hands in the ordinary course of their work.

278 Amongst the 128 injuries caused by sharp edges, only one was not to the hands and, on the face of it, all 127 could have been prevented by wearing heavy leather gloves. But 63 hand injuries resulted from handling components which were being placed into or removed from tools or jigs and, in the majority of these cases, heavy gloves would have been a serious hindrance or made the movement impossible. Cotton gloves are worn, particularly by people on strip fed machines, where hindrance to movement is not critical, but they provide only limited protection and they do not last as well as leather. Oil soaked cotton gloves are often used as a means of smearing oil onto the surface of metal about to be pressed. We understand this method of lubrication carries a high dermatitis risk but no-one has succumbed and, presumably even these oil soaked gloves have prevented several small cuts to the hands.

Table 10 – Agents of injury in the gear section

Agent of injury	Number of injuries
SWARF	0
MATERIAL AND COMPONENT	
Cut by sharp edge when handling	1
MACHINES AND TOOLS	
Nipped in hand operated press	1
Hand on power driven wire brush	1
Hand on power driven grinding wheel	2
Component spun whilst drilling it (setter)	1
Wire fragment in eye from powered wire brush	1
Cut on gear-cutting wheel during adjustment	1
BOXES	
Bruised hand	1
PASSAGEWAY	
Fall	1
OTHER	
Cut on nail projecting from scrap wood	1
TOTAL	11

279 By contrast with the lathes and presses, accidents on the gear-cutting section are very few, although the number of people working there is more than half as many as on the lathes. The classic accident of someone having his fingers taken into the inrunning nip between a cutter and component has not materialised on these machines, although they are not guarded in a way which would fully comply with statute. It so happens that one operator looks after several semi-automatic machines and never approaches the dangerous parts until they have stopped. Uncovenanted re-starting of a machine when an operator is attending to the dangerous parts has not occurred. Out of 11 accidents which we have recorded for the present population, only two were concerned directly with gear-cutting and both of these resulted from contact with sharp-edged wheels (one a component and one an unmounted cutter). We think it significant that the components cut on these machines are small and most of the people working here have years of experience. Six out of the 11 accidents have occurred on machines other than gear-cutters. Two occurred on a grinding wheel; this was before our suggested modification was made to the guard. Two occurred on a power driven wire brush, for which we have not been able to make a specific suggestion, although wearing safety spectacles would obviously have stopped the eye injury.

P. I. POWELL
CAROLINE WARNE

Appendix 8
Evidence of job specificity

280 We found that all jobs had inherent risks of injury specific to them. The number and severity of these risks influenced the accident rates.

Accident rates for the machine and assembly shops
281 The average number of accidents per person over the 21 months we studied was 1·7 for the assembly shop and 2·2 for the machine shop. These figures do not take into account the experience of the people in these shops, but the machine shop had a larger core of experienced workers than the assembly shop and so, on the basis of experience alone, might be expected to have a lower accident rate. However, the machine shop had a higher accident rate than the assembly shop, which we think was due to the greater risks involved in the type of work performed.

Accident rates in the machine shop sections
282 We calculated the average number of accidents per person over our study period for each of the eight machine shop sections. This was done first for the people who had been in the machine shop for the whole of the period studied (the stable population), and then for everyone who had been working in the machine shop at any time during our study. This second set of rates does not take account of the length of time people had worked in a particular section. The results are shown below.

Table 11 – Average number of accidents per person in the machine shop sections

Section	Average accidents/person in 21 months.	
	Stable population	Total population
Lathes	6·1	3·9
Power presses	5·5	2·7
Grinders	4·8	2·6
Drills	4·6	2·2
Milling machines	2·2	1·6
Gear-cutters	1·2	0·8
Inspection	0·9	0·7

283 The results show wide variations in the accident rates between different sections. The rates for the total population are lower than for the stable population, because many of those included had not worked in the section for very long and this was not allowed for, i.e., everyone was treated as if he had worked 21 months. The rank order of accident rates for the different sections is the same for both the stable and the total population. Since the number of inexperienced people differs in different sections, it seems that the difference between the sections in terms of the work factors overrides experience factors.

Accident rates of foremen, chargehands and setters

284 The numbers of foremen, chargehands and setters were small, and so we calculated their accident rates per 100 man days worked for greater accuracy. Accident rates were calculated for the rest of the men and also for the women in the machine shop who had been in our study the whole time, using the same method so that they could be compared. The rates obtained are shown in the table.

Table 12 – Accident rates of foremen, chargehands and setters, compared with rates for men and women in the machine shop

	No. of people	Accidents per 100 man days
Foremen	5	0·42 *
Chargehands	4	0·53 *
Setters	27	0·90
Machine shop men (stable)	65	0·98
Machine shop women (stable)	45	0·88
Total machine shop	110	0·94

The rates for foremen and chargehands cannot be considered reliable in view of the small numbers involved.

285 The foremen, chargehands and setters are all people of long experience in the machine shop and so it seemed more logical to compare them with the stable machine shop population rather than the whole machine shop. The foremen and chargehands have low rates compared to the rest of the machine shop. This can be explained by their being less exposed to risk than the operators, as they do a fair amount of paper work and only occasionally operate or set machines. The setters' accident rate is similar to that of the operators, but the setters sustain different kinds of accidents.

JEAN MARTIN

Appendix 9
Notes on job specificity

– and some related effects, including the difficulty of finding adequate control groups in the practical situation.

286 Accident research suffers from two difficulties in the matter of gathering statistical data.

287 The first is that if the source of the data is factory records, the data will probably be incomplete, and not in a convenient form. The second is that if, in order to get complete data, you transfer the research to the laboratory, the results may not be valid for the practical situation or, as we find in the current research, other things are far *more* important.

288 The typical instance of the first difficulty is that of using factory records to measure the number of accidents taking place in the factory. Even the best of factories does not record more than about two-thirds of the minor injuries, in our experience, and it can also miss recording lost-time injuries. Buzzard and Radforth (1964) have explained some of the anomalies of factory record systems and Chapanis (1967) has detailed the ways in which the results of laboratory experiments become inapplicable to the practical situation.

Occupational groupings
289 Most systems for classifying accidents are based on groupings of occupation which appear to have some 'a priori' similarity. Thus there is a temptation to make groups such as 'assembly workers', 'lathe operators', 'electricians', and so on. The underlying assumption is that, by and large, these groups of people are doing work in which, over the course of the time during which data has been gathered, the exposure to risk of an accident is the same. Sometimes a statistical analysis will be based on this assumption and conclusions are drawn about the propensity of individuals within the group to have accidents. This assumption is false because it ignores a whole range of technical causes contributing to the accident. Here are some examples of technical factors which influence the accident situation.

290 **Nominally identical machines are not identical.** Each part of a machine is made to within certain dimensional limits and the resulting machines, although they may look identical, do not feel the same to the operator working them. During their working lives, they wear in different ways and have different things done to them by way of maintenance. The result is that, if you walk down a line of apparently 'identical' machines in a factory and try working them, one after the other, you will find that one control handle on machine A feels more stiff than that of machine B and again less stiff than that of machine C and so on. On a more mundane level, you will no doubt have observed the same effect when driving a friend's car, which is nominally exactly the same model as your own.

291 The differences in adjustment and consequent 'feel' of the controls of a machine can contribute to errors by the operator in two ways. Firstly, if he changes from working one machine to another, he will tend to make mistakes in the degree of force and the amount of movement required on a control handle to produce a given effect within the machine. Secondly, he will become fatigued in a different way, depending on what particular physical or mental effort he finds most tiring to maintain. You will know what I mean by this if you have driven a similar car to your own but with the clutch adjusted very much tighter or the brakes or the steering more slack. You have to anticipate your use of these controls in a quite different way to that to which you are accustomed on your own car. Further, when you get back to your own car, it feels odd, but, of course, the effect wears off more quickly because you are much more used to driving your own car than your friend's.

292 Machines have things added to them, which limit the jobs done on them. In one row of nominally identical machines in one of the factories we are studying, some machines have collet guards of one shape and others of a different shape; some machines are equipped with a multiple jet for supplying oil to the area where metal cutting is done and other machines are equipped with a single jet, or none; some machines have their oil sumps filled with oil and yet others have their sumps filled with water containing a small proportion of water soluble lubricant. Some machines have a damaged oil supply system and are used for jobs which can be cut without oil; on some machines the guides of the tool saddle have become worn and hence this machine cannot be used where tools mounted on the saddle are required to cut to very fine limits of accuracy (in other words, the machine needs some attention and, in time, it will get it, but meanwhile it is used for a particular class of job where high accuracy is not required); some machines are the favourites of particular operators, because they have got more used to them than any other and are able to work faster on them. On some machines the local lighting has broken down and these machines are therefore not suitable for high accuracy work (again, this is something which will be put right by the maintenance department eventually but, in the meantime, there is a selection of work done on this machine); some machines are quicker and easier to set up for particular jobs than others because of small modifications which have been done to some of the tool holders in the past, so again, there is a selection of jobs done on these machines which is different from those done on the others.

293 The result is that, on this row of nominally identical machines, only a selection of the available work is done on each. Like people, the machines become specialised. Furthermore, the operators become specialised, but this is dealt with in another section below.

294   Each job done on the machine carries its own special risks. One of the work-shops we are studying deals with a variety of small metal components. These include sheet-steel cases, plates and discs, pressed out of the flat and sometimes further drilled with various holes; and steel spindles, some of them no thicker than a darning needle. The edges of the sheet-steel raw material and of the components pressed out of it, are often extremely sharp; they present a finger-cutting hazard to anyone who has to handle them. Spindles can also present hazards; we knew of one piercing someone's foot.

295   In the drilling section, the girls working the drills are subject to a variety of risks, each peculiar to the component she is working on and to the particular operation she has to perform on it. If she has to handle a sheet-steel component with sharp edges, she is quite likely to cut her fingers, sooner or later. If she has to drill a hole in a very small component, and is obliged to hold the component whilst it is under the drill, she may slightly misplace her finger when drilling the umpteenth component and drill finger instead of metal. When drilling cast components, there is always the risk of the drill suddenly breaking through into a hidden blowhole and the operator subsequently losing control of the casting.

296   To return to the small capstan lathes mentioned earlier, here too there is a similar connection between particular risks and particular machining operations. For example, brass is usually cut dry and the swarf from the cutting operation breaks into splinters which fly about. These small particles of metal are so light in weight that their impact on the human body does no injury, except if they hit an eye. If you will accept for a moment that only certain operators do the dry jobs on brass, for reasons which will be explained more fully later, then it follows that not all the operators of this seemingly identical set of machines are subject to risk of foreign body in the eye.

297   Another risk associated with the material is associated with the cutting of special steels, such as stainless. Certain steels produce swarf like coarse flexible string which is often quite difficult to break and the operator of the lathe cutting this material has to guide the swarf away from the cutting tool into the swarf tray. If she touches the swarf, there is a high risk of cutting the fingers, since it has very sharp edges. We have also come across components, some of which had a sharp edge on one end if the previous machining done on that had been inaccurate but a blunt edge if the machining had been done correctly. An operator handling hundreds of these components, most of which have been machined correctly, occasionally fingered a bad one and often cut herself when doing so.

Self-selection by operators, and the effect of setter selection
298   In one of the workshops we are studying, there is an underlying system of self-selection of jobs. The factory is engaged in batch production, the batches varying in size from a few hundred to several thousand. There is a bonus system which rewards the operator for producing components faster than a particular rate fixed by a time-study done in the past. New recruits are attached to a section for a probationary period of six weeks, in which time they are expected to become

accustomed to doing the job sufficiently well that they can thereafter earn bonus payment. There is no training, as such. A new operator will be introduced to a machine by the foreman or the setter, usually the latter, who will demonstrate a particular job, watch the operator do it a few times and then leave him or her to get on with it with little more than an occasional visit to check that all appears to be well. In this way, the operator will 'have a go' at such variety of jobs as the setter thinks fit. His choice depends on what jobs he has available to do on the section at that particular time and on his opinion of the operator's ability. For the operator, the goal is to work fast enough to earn the socially acceptable percentage of bonus. If, towards the end of the probationary period, an operator finds he cannot work with sufficient speed, he may decide to transfer to some other department or to leave the factory altogether, or the section foreman will come to a similar decision. The effect is the same in that the operator ceases to do that particular sort of work. Thus, all operators with more than six weeks' experience on any section are people who have proved that they are capable of working at a particular speed on a selection of jobs. Thereafter, they may enlarge the repertoire of jobs which they do, but this again depends on what jobs become available and which operator the setter chooses to do a particular job. The relationship between setter and operator is, therefore, crucial. A setter may get favourites, to whom he may direct all the 'plum' jobs. An operator may make a mess of, or express a dislike for a particular job and thereafter not get it again. The phenomenon we often see is that certain operators become 'star turns' at particular jobs and they will then have those jobs directed to them on future occasions.

299 In these various ways, each person in a section becomes subject to a particular variety of risks. No two operators are subject to identical risks over a long period of time, in our experience, because they never do an identical mixture of tasks on the same machine with the same components. Hence, we were unable to find exact matches for experimental controls. The best we could do was to match certain characteristics for the instant of time at which an accident took place. These characteristics were – the type of task, the type of machine, and the material and general shape of the component.

300 In the above, we have confined our examples to the situation in the machine shop, because this is where the effect is more obvious. However, it also took place in our assembly shop, where operators of high ability could be found doing any one of several dozen different tasks and the best of them would be reject operators, that is people who could right the mistakes in assembly of anyone else. At the other extreme, the slow learners would be found doing only one of half a dozen different tasks, year in and year out. As in the machine shop, there was a constant change of details on the components handled, as different models were completed, batch by batch.

301 Only in the despatch department did we find a certain homogeneity of task among certain groups of workers over a long period of time. Thus, it was in the despatch department that we were able to prove the overall relationship between the amount of work done by the group of people and the number of accidents they sustained. And by careful observation of the mixture of parcels handled, we were able to show the relationship between the risks associated with particular types of parcel and the accidents sustained by the people handling them. Further, we were able to obtain descriptive data about individual handling methods and the effect this had on individual accident rates.

302 So what are our conclusions from all this? First, the factory situation is complicated and the separation of the effects of various factors which cause accidents is difficult.

303 Secondly, human factors, such as the skill of the individual operator, tend to be obscured, because the operator does a different mixture of work to that of his differently skilful colleague.

304 Thirdly, where machines are used to help do the work, the variations in these (despite their superficially identical appearance), introduce a number of further factors which are difficult to measure.

305 Fourthly, where machines are used, they make a contribution to the work output and the true work output of the individual operator is so bound up with that of the machine that a true measure of the combined worker/machine output is not a comparative measure of the work done by individual operators.

306 Fifthly, homogeneity of work, even over a period of time, is rare in the industrial situation, and we think this explains the conflicting research findings about the effect of human factors on accidents. For example, in the Industrial Fatigue Research Board Report No. 34, 1926 by Newbold, he said that the average number of accidents was much influenced by a comparatively small number of workers and that the distribution (of accidents) among the workers was far from chance. In the light of our experience, this finding could be explained purely in terms of the uneven distribution of high-risk jobs. But, as you will see from other parts of our report, it was probably also influenced by job changing (the effect of inexperience) and the propensity of some people to have every trivial injury dressed by the surgery, whilst others behaved differently. Indeed, Newbold himself found that the people who have most accidents are, on the whole, those who pay most visits to the ambulance room for minor sickness. If he had said 'The people who *report* most accidents . . . ', he might have been nearer the mark, in the industrial situation he was using for his experiment. Buzzard, Whitfield and Keatinge, among others, have drawn attention to this same point. We found in our machine shop that high scores of minor accidents were no guide to the incidence of major accidents. Each situation differs. If the risks are all of minor injury, no major injury will be likely to result – such was the case in most of our assembly shop tasks. In lathe work, repetition of foreign bodies in the eye is obviously going to result in a nasty one, sooner or later. There is no general rule, but a safety officer with intimate knowledge of the work processes of his own factory can quickly see if minor accident repetition is serious by *going to have a look at the process concerned*. This is the vital step. Hence the need for factory records of minor injury analysed by areas. P. I. POWELL

Appendix 10
Accidents and work done

ASSEMBLY AND MACHINE SHOPS

307 We found it difficult to obtain measures of work done in the assembly and machine shops. Overall production figures were too imprecise, as they do not allow for the variety of components produced, some of which required more machines and more tasks than others. Further, both individual and overall production figures have no relationship with the different risks inherent in systems of work. The major factors of shop, section, machine, component, task and operator contributed in different ways and to varying extents to each accident. No one situation was strictly comparable with another (see Appendix, para. 280 *et seq.*).

308 However, we did study three factors which had some association with work done to see if we could trace any patterns.

Accidents and electricity consumption
309 We found that a sample chart of the electricity consumed mainly by the machine shop showed a higher current in the morning than in the afternoon. There were more accidents in the former period. However, electricity consumption has no relation to the risks of the jobs for which the electricity is consumed and it can only be a very general measure of work done. Appendix 21, para. 483, discusses the hour-to-hour effects in more detial.

Accidents and bonus pay
310 We examined the possibility of using weekly bonus figures as a measure of the work done. In the assembly shop this was not possible, because the sub-assembly section had individual bonuses. In the machine shop the work was unpaced and we thought that the effort a person put into his job might be reflected in the bonus he earned. The bonus system was based on a count of pieces of product produced per hour. We related a sample of bonus figures in the machine shop for 20 weeks chosen at random (after excluding weeks with incomplete observation) with the number of accidents which occurred in those weeks. The correlation obtained (Spearman's rho $=0·085$) was not significant.

311 However, we had found that accident rates fluctuated according to the number of new recruits present (see Appendix para. 342). We thought that this might be contaminating the result, as new recruits tended to earn less bonus and have more accidents. We repeated the analysis considering only those people who were there during the whole of our study period, but the correlation obtained (Spearman's rho $= 0.036$) was again not significant.

312 We conclude that bonus earnings are not related to work done for two reasons. First, a count of pieces of product per hour is not a measure of the human work content. On some tasks it was easy to earn a high rate of bonus and on others it was difficult to earn even a modest bonus. On some of the more automated processes the bonus earned was almost entirely governed by the machine speed. The operator could do little to increase his bonus earnings apart from seeing that the raw material supply was replenished and trusting that the machine would not break down. Where the effort of production is shared between a person and a machine, a detailed analysis of the person's task is necessary, rather than a simple count of production.

313 Secondly, we discovered semi-official systems aimed at maintaining bonus earnings at a steady rate. Tasks were 'good' or 'bad' according to the ease with which high bonus could be earned. On the records of work done, there was a tendency for the hours taken on a good task to be extended and on a bad task to be reduced in compensation. Records of the weekly bonus earned by individuals were scanned by the appropriate supervisor, who then tried to arrange good jobs for those with low bonus in a preceding week.

314 Thus, bonus pay is unlikely to correlate with accidents in the general industrial situation because many bonus systems take little account of the effort required for a task, and no account of the risks involved in that task.

Accidents and rate of working
315 We knew the rate of working that had been fixed by the work study department for a large number of jobs in both shops. We had hoped to be able to compare this with the actual rate of working at the time of an accident, but managed to obtain the information in only a small number of cases. This was because the only people able to give a reliable numerical figure to their output were those on automatic machines set at a specific rate.

316 We asked people whether they thought they were working below, at, or above the fixed rate, but decided that the subjective nature of this information was not very reliable.

317 We were therefore unable to carry out any analysis on rate of working at the time of an accident.

DESPATCH DEPARTMENT

318 We had three measures of the work done by the men in the sample at the despatch department. Two were obtained directly from the department's own records, and one was developed by us for more specific purposes during the study. We related the measures to accidents.

319 There were three occupational categories at this shop. Most of the men worked in groups of four or five, made up of two 'sorters' and two or three 'barrow-men'. The sorters received and destination-coded the goods and the barrowmen moved the goods to the outgoing vans and put them on. The third category, 'van-packers', worked mainly individually. They checked that goods were in the correct vans and packed each van evenly.

Accidents and weight handled
320 From the records kept by the department we recorded the weight of goods handled by each working group for each day of our study. We also collected information about the membership of each group, the number of hours worked, and details of any other kinds of work the group did, e.g., sweeping the work-place. The total weight handled by the groups indirectly applied to the van-packers, as all the goods were transported to them by the groups.

321 We calculated the total weight handled in the department each calendar month, standardised to a base of 20 working days per month. The accident rate in the department was calculated on this same monthly basis. We tested the relationship between weight and accidents and found that it was not statistically significant. We think this was because the types of goods most likely to cause injury were in fact those of the lightest weight, and thus it was more likely that there would be an inverse relationship when the factors were studied more specifically.

322 Therefore we calculated the average daily weight of the goods handled by each of 26 sorters during our study. We had data only for the total weight handled by each group, each day, but from our observations we felt able to assume that the two sorters working together in a group handled approximately the same weight. We ranked the sorters for the average weight of goods they handled, and tested the relationship between this and their accident rate rank order. Using Kendall's tau, we found no relationship.

323 We thought that the lack of any relationship might be due to the system of work which allowed some sorters to obtain higher weight loads with lower risk of accident (see Appendix 30). We therefore excluded ten sorters who handled the highest weight loads, and found that there was a positive relationship (Kendall's tau = 0·22) significant at the 0·02 level between the other 16 sorters' average daily tonnage and accident rates.

324 We went on to compare the accidents of the ten sorters who handled the highest weight loads with the accidents of the ten who handled the lowest. We found that the former group sustained fewer accidents (Kendall's tau = −0·33). The relationship was significant at the 0·02 level.

Accidents and volume of goods despatched
325 We noted the number of vans despatched each day and to what capacity

each van was filled. The vans were nearly all of standard dimensions, so that was a measure of the volume of goods despatched.

326 We felt that the number of packages handled was likely to be more related to risk than the weight. Unfortunately it was impossible to count the number each man handled, but, when dealing with the department as a whole, the total volume despatched per month was an approximate measure of the number of packages handled per month.

327 We calculated the total volume despatched per calendar month, standardising to a base of 20 days per month (as we had done before with the weight calculations). We tested volume against accidents per month (Kendall's tau = 0·462), and found a significant relationship at the 0·01 level. This relationship is illustrated below.

Figure 1   Relationship between volume of goods despatched and accidents

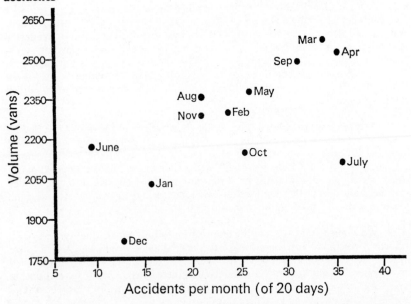

The result showed that total accidents were related to volume of goods despatched.

Accidents and type of package handled

328 It was clear that some types of packages were more likely to cause injury than others. For this reason we sampled the packages for 16 weeks to find what types of goods were handled. We wanted to find how many of each type were handled, and by whom they were handled. We classified the goods into seven categories. These were:

(a) Tea chests.

(b) Other wooden chests.

(c) Cardboard cartons, secured with metal bands.

(d) Cardboard cartons, secured with wire bands.

(e) Cardboard cartons, secured otherwise, e.g., adhesive tape, plastic bands, string.

(f) Other parcels.

(g) Other general goods, e.g., drums, lengths of wood, cylinders.

329 We sampled by observing each sorter for 15 minutes each week, noting down the number he handled of each type of package. Thus we obtained numerical information about the types of package handled by each sorter, and by the department as a whole, over a period of five months.

330 We analysed the proportions of each type of package each week and found that they did not vary significantly from week to week, although the quantity of work varied seasonally (see Appendix para. 446).

331 We calculated the number of each type of goods that entered the department from our sample of over 10,000 individual goods items. We also calculated the number of accidents contributed to by the goods of each category, i.e., accidents where the agent of injury was a goods item. The results are shown below:

Table 13 – Type of package and numbers of accidents

Type of package	Number sampled entering department	Percentage entering department	Number of occasions where package was agent of injury	Percentage of occasions where package was agent of injury
Tea chests	584	5·7%	62	28·8%
Metal bands	965	9·4%	53	24·7%
Other goods	692	6·7%	39	18·1%
Other wooden chests	371	3·6%	29	13·5%
Other cartons	6,110	59·4%	18	8·4%
Wire bands	807	7·8%	11	5·1%
Other parcels	760	7·4%	3	1·4%
TOTAL	10,289	100·0%	215	100·0%

332 The results indicate that tea chests, other wooden chests, metal banded cartons and other goods offered the greatest potential for injury. Although these types of goods entered the department in small proportions (25 per cent in total), they were the agent of injury in over 85 per cent of the accidents we discovered where goods were the agent of injury.

333 Nearly all the tea chests contained light plastic goods. The chests were of standard dimensions, but such that they were awkward to manoeuvre (19 in. × 19 in. × 24 in.). We observed that the men usually grasped a chest with one hand under a bottom corner and the other hand over an opposite top corner. Each corner and edge were bound with a metal strip, but after much usage (empty tea chests were returned and re-used) the strips began to tear and split away from the sides of the chest. This increased the risk of injury, particularly to the hands, wrists and arms, because the torn and protruding metal had very sharp edges. Sorters, particularly, working in the confined space of a van, often had little chance of seeing the risk. The chests gradually got into worse condition, for although they were marked 'Fragile', they were regularly thrown about by the men, who let go and dropped them in order to avoid having to adjust the position of their hands on the sharp edges when lowering them.

334 The metal bands used to secure cardboard cartons were very sharp-edged $\frac{1}{2}$ in. strips of metal, which were often loose owing to faulty connection. A few men were observed lifting cartons by the metal bands, which obviously increased the risk of injury. Even when handled by grasping the edges or corners of a carton, men would still accidentally touch the metal bands from time to time and cut themselves.

335 From our sampling data we calculated the number of tea chests and metal banded cartons handled by each sorter, expressed as a percentage of all types of goods handled. We related each sorter's exposure to tea chests and metal banded cartons with the number of accidents they had sustained where one or other of these two types of goods was the agent of injury. Using the Mann Whitney U-test, we found that sorters with two or more such accidents had handled significantly more tea chests and metal banded cartons than sorters with none or only one such accident ($p < 0.05$).

336 We may therefore conclude that accidents where these goods were the agent of injury were related to the victim's exposure to the risks inherent in the goods.

337 We confirmed the dominating influence of these two types of goods on the sorters' accidents by testing the relationship between the total accidents sustained throughout the study and the percentage of tea chests and metal banded cartons handled. Using the Mann Whitney U-test, we found that sorters with high accident rates had handled significantly more tea chests and metal banded cartons than sorters with low accident rates ($p < 0.05$).

338 'Other wooden chests' and 'other goods' were also the agent of injury in a disproportionate number of accidents. However, we did not feel it would be reasonable to do a similar analysis on the sorter's exposure to these goods, because they were so varied in size, weight and quality.

JEAN MARTIN, M. SIMON

Appendix 11
Experience

Length of service

339 In the assembly and machine shops, we compared the length of service in the company of the victims with their first controls, using Wilcoxon's Matched Pairs Signed Ranks Test. The results are shown below:

Table 14 – Length of service – victims and first controls

Group	Number in group	Significance level
Machine shop men	195	0·006
Machine shop women	115	0·02
Assembly shop women	220	0·001

These results show that for all three groups the victims had significantly shorter length of service than their first controls.

340 In the mill, we compared the length of service of people with several accidents with that of matched pairs of people with fewer or no accidents, using the Mann Whitney U-Test. The high accident people had significantly shorter lengths of service than the low accident people ($p < 0·001$).

341 In the despatch department, most people had several years' service and analysis showed nothing significant. It was in any case largely a matter of comparing people with 20 years' service with people of five years' service.

Recruitment and accidents

342 In the assembly and machine shops, we correlated the number of accidents which occurred each month with the number of people recruited that month, using Spearman's rho. A value of rho of 0·53 was obtained which is significant at the 0·01 level. A second correlation was calculated considering only the accidents of those people who had been in the shop for less than six months. The value of rho obtained was 0·77, which is also significant at the 0·01 level. The figure overleaf illustrates this latter relationship.

343 These results show that the people present with only a short experience

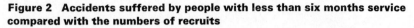

Figure 2   Accidents suffered by people with less than six months service compared with the numbers of recruits

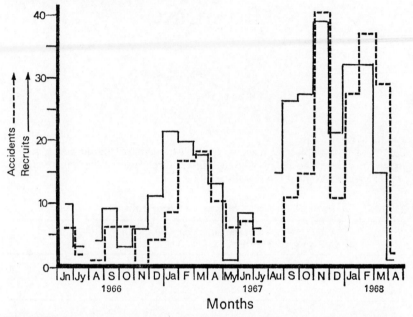

are very important in determining the overall accident rate.* In the mill and the despatch department, there was not enough recruitment to affect the overall accident rates.

Specific task experience
344 In the assembly and machine shops, we classified specific task experience into six categories of occasions spent doing the task before. We defined the categories as follows:

Never

Rarely –   not more than once in six months, or less than three times altogether;

Occasionally –   less than once a week, but more than once every six months;

_____

* We were asked to calculate the accident rate for people with, for example, 2 months experience and compare it with the rate for the permanent population. This would be invalid because someone with 2 months experience in, say, Jan/Feb 1966 cannot be grouped with someone else with 2 months experience in, say, June/July 1967, because the work and environmental conditions will not have been the same.

Often –	more than once a week. This applied particularly to people who rotated between 2 or 3 tasks;
Usually –	most of the time;
Always –	(includes people who did one task as long as the supply of components lasted).

345 We compared the number of times the tasks of the accident victims and first controls fell into each task experience category. We found that task experience of the victims was significantly less than that of the first controls i.e., it fell significantly more often into one of the three short experience categories of never, rarely and occasionally than into the three longer experience categories, and the task experience of their first controls fell the other way round. This was true for the three groups; machine shop men, machine shop women and assembly shop women.

346 In the mill, we used the same six categories. The task experience of the victims was distributed as follows:

Always, usually or often 105
Occasionally, rarely or never 189

347 It was not possible to relate these figures to the actual frequency with which tasks fell into the six categories, but most of the tasks in this shop appeared to come up regularly and task experience generally fell into the usually or often categories. Thus, it appears that more accidents occurred on tasks on which people had less experience. It was usually impossible in this shop to fulfil the criteria for a first control, because the jobs were so varied, and therefore we could not compare the task experience of victims and first controls.

348 In the despatch department, all the men handled a variety of goods and were, in effect, on the same task all the time. It was impossible for us to obtain measures of specific task experience that were related to occasions spent handling certain types of goods.

Relationship between accidents and number of task changes
349 In the machine shop, weekly work sheets were kept which recorded all the tasks each person performed during the week. We obtained work sheets for eight months and took a sample of ten sheets for each person whose accidents had been observed for the whole of our study. Records were obtained for 70 operators altogether. No records were available for the setters, and the milling section was omitted from the analysis as records were available for only three people.

350 We calculated the average number of tasks per week for each of the remaining 67 people. Using Spearman's rho, we tested the relationship between the average number of tasks per week and the number of accidents each person had at work, treating each of the machine shop sections separately. The results are shown below:

Table 15 – Correlation of accidents and average number of tasks per week for the machine shop sections

Section	Number of people	Rho	Significance
Press	20	0·60	0·01
Grinding	10	0·77	0·01
Drills	13	0·59	0·05
Gears	10	0·57	0·05
Microns	8	0·48	n/s
Capstans	6	0·58	n/s

351 All the sections showed a trend towards an association between number of accidents and average number of tasks per week but the results were significant only for the larger sections.

352 We decided to combine the results from the different sections, controlling for the differences in accident rates and average numbers of tasks in the different sections. Each section was split into high and low accident people with equal numbers in each half. (It was necessary to eliminate some people in the middle on a random basis to achieve this.) The high accident people and the low accident people from all the sections were combined and the average number of tasks per week of the high accident people was compared with that of the low accident people using a Mann Whitney U-Test. Having equal numbers of people from each section in the two groups eliminated the differences in the number of task changes between the different sections. Choosing high and low accident people from within the sections controlled for the different accident rates in different sections. Sixty records were analysed in this way, seven being eliminated to give equal numbers. A U value of 612 was obtained which is significant at the 1 per cent level. This shows that the relationship between accidents and average numbers of tasks per week holds independently of section, which affects both of these measures.

353 Number of task changes is a measure of experience rather than of work load. Because someone has more changes of task in a week than another, it does not mean that he is doing any more work, but it does mean that his specific task experience will be less.

354 In the assembly shop, we were unable to show a relationship between accidents and task changes, because the factory did not keep individual records of task for this shop and we did not have the time to do more than a weekly sample. We looked at the tasks and task changes for a group of high accident and a group of low accident people. In both groups we found several people who changed tasks a lot, but the high accident people were usually changing amongst high risk tasks and the low accident people were changing amongst low risk tasks.* It was not possible to separate the effect on the accident rate of frequent task changes from the risks associated with the different tasks.

355 Over a period of 11 weeks in the mill, the number of changes of task were recorded for a sample of five pairs of people, one of each pair having a high and the other a low number of accidents, but both doing the same job. For three of the pairs, the high accident people had at least twice as many changes of task as the low accident people, but the other two pairs showed no significant differences. Clearly no definite conclusions can be drawn from such a small sample and unfortunately the data were not readily available to extend the sample.

Time on the task
356 In the assembly and machine shops, we compared the length of time the victims and first controls had been working on their tasks at the time of the accident, using Wilcoxon's Matched Pairs Signed Ranks Test. The results were significant for the men in the machine shop ($p=6\%$, $N=94$) but not the women. From the frequency distribution, we thought that there might be a significant difference in time on the task in the first hour when most accidents occurred for women in the assembly shop. We therefore compared time on the task for victims and first controls when both had worked for less than an hour on that task. There were, however, only a few such cases where the victim and first control differed in how long they had been on the task. Of these, the victims had been on the task for less time than the first control, but owing to the small sample this difference was not statistically significant. The results suggest that people are more likely to have accidents during the beginning of a period on a task.

357 In the mill, we looked at the distribution of accidents in terms of which quarter of a task the accident occurred in. We used quarters, as opposed to actual time on the task, to control for jobs which differed a great deal in duration. The number of accidents falling in the four quarters were as follows:

First quarter	60
Second quarter	20
Third quarter	16
Last quarter	55

358 A χ^2 test showed that accidents were significantly differently distributed over the four quarters ($p < 0.001$). Inspection shows that accidents occur more in the first and last quarters of the task.

359 Although the task content did not vary from quarter to quarter, situations which might contribute to accidents were more likely to occur in the first and

---

* Examples of high risk tasks were the handling of sharp-edged parts, the use of heated tools, the forceful use of a screwdriver either for rotary driving or as a lever.
Examples of low risk tasks were the assembly and lubrication of small parts, where it was seldom necessary to use any large physical force.

last quarters. For example, if a machine was not set up quite correctly, something was more likely to go wrong at the beginning of a task. At the beginning and end of tasks, the piles of metal were larger, which increased the risk of them toppling, and also meant that great care was necessary while stacking them.

JEAN MARTIN

Appendix 12
Age and experience structures in the four shops

360 We examined the distribution of age and experience in the machine and assembly shops at the beginning, middle and end of the study, to see if either had changed appreciably.

361 The age structure showed no significant changes between these times in either the machine or the assembly shops and neither did the experience distribution in the machine shop. In the assembly shop there was a rise in the number of inexperienced people in the middle of the study because of increased recruitment.

362 Similar analyses in the despatch department and the mill revealed no significant variations in either age or experience throughout the period of the studies.

JEAN MARTIN

Appendix 13
Appreciation of risks at work

363 People in any working environment are exposed to risks of injury, from many sources. A considerable number could be removed by better machine design and layout, but sometimes this is not feasible, for reasons of economy or speed of work. In such cases, it is particularly important that the operator be drilled in a safe working method, which keeps him away from contact with danger. The safe method will often be slower and more complex than the one the operator would follow if left to his own devices. Under the pressure of a piece rate or bonus system the operator will be tempted to take short cuts, despite the risks, to earn a higher wage. It is therefore important that operators should be alerted to the risks inherent in their work, and in the short cuts they might be tempted to make. This alerting should reinforce the learning of the safe working methods by providing some tangible reason for them.

364 Much safety propaganda is directed towards this sort of approach, but before trying to influence people's opinions it is wise to know what these opinions are. What follows is a description of a short study which set out to discover this.

365 During observation of work in a light engineering factory, I was collecting details of the jobs being done, and of the risks involved in them. This entailed going round and watching operators at work, and noting down the risks of injury that I could see in the job. At the same time, without showing my own notes, I asked the operator his, or her, opinion of the risk. The question I used was: 'How is it possible to hurt yourself doing this job?' I noted down the replies, clarifying them, if necessary, by further questioning. If the operator had not mentioned all the risks which I had noted down, I then pointed them out to him, and asked his opinion of them. Some 200 jobs were treated in this way and about 80 operators were questioned.

366 From the replies it was clear that the question was usually treated as though it had been: 'How have you, or someone you know, been hurt doing this job?' For example, two operators doing very similar work on adjacent centreless grinders gave different assessments of the risks involved. Both were placing small components between the two wheels of the grinder, and then pressing a lever to bring the wheels together, but only one mentioned the risk

(Reproduced from NIIP Bulletin, Spring 1969)

of the safety device on the machine failing, so that the wheels came together with the operator's hand between them. It turned out that just such an accident had happened to this operator, but not to the other.

367 Most of the risks mentioned by the operators would result in injuries serious enough to need first-aid treatment. They were nearly all risks which they had succumbed to themselves, or seen quite frequently, and they were more commonly connected with the component being handled, than with the machine being operated. Most operators considered only the risks associated with their normal method of work, not mentioning those due to machine failure, or incorrect ways of working. Thus the risks most commonly mentioned in this factory were cuts from sharp edges of sheet metal, the dangers of flying swarf from lathes, and strain from lifting heavy boxes, or operating awkward controls.

368 The risks noted by the observer, but seldom or not at all by the operators, fell into three groups.

369 First, there were risks producing only trivial injuries, such as scratches from swarf, or small cuts and bruises from handling awkward metal components. These were only mentioned by operators if they produced injuries very frequently, otherwise they were dismissed as the price to be paid for a good bonus.

370 Secondly, there were risks which very rarely produce injury. These were mainly risks associated with the machine being operated, and they included the well-known, serious risks such as catching hair or sleeves in moving drills, or fingernails in the collets of lathes, or trapping the fingers between the cutters of automatic gear-cutting machines. These risks were mentioned by only a few operators, mainly with little experience, perhaps because they had been pointed out fairly recently during training. When the risks were mentioned to the more experienced operators, it was apparent that they were aware of them, but did not think them worth worrying about. Some operators considered that they would have to be so stupid, clumsy, or absent-minded to succumb, that it could never happen to them. Others thought that there was nothing they could do about it, so why worry? As one said, 'It is just part of the job, which you have to accept, so why worry yourself sick over it'?

371 Thirdly, there were risks stemming from incidents outside the normal pattern of work, for example the failure of machine guards or interlocks. These were either regarded as too unlikely to be worth bothering about, or their existence was denied altogether. For example, one woman operator was reaming a small hole in a metal component, which she had to offer up to the moving reamer. This is a job in which, if the reamer misses the hole, it can slip across the component, and gouge a hole in the side of the operator's finger. I had seen several accidents from this cause, and when this operator did not mention the risk, I pointed it out to her. She replied that she had done many thousands of these components, without ever hurting herself, and that it was not possible to do so. She then proceeded to demonstrate her point, before I could stop her, by making the reamer slip several times. To my intense relief it missed her finger each time, but by a distance of only a few millimetres.

372 Not one operator mentioned the risks involved in forgetting to replace covers over moving parts, for example, over the chucks of drills, or the bar advance of small lathes; nor was any mention made of risks involved in taking short cuts in the laid down methods of work. But I had seen several instances of both of these practices.*

373 There were great differences between the risks mentioned by different operators, even when working on the same job. For example, of two women working on a power operated riveting machine, one could see only the risk of straining her back from the awkward operating position, while the other came out with a long list which included the danger of riveting her finger if the machine guard of the machine failed. This second operator had, however, never seen, nor heard of such an accident taking place. Obviously different people vary in their tendency to see risks in a given situation. The variables underlying such differences need much deeper investigation.

374 It was possible from the study to define some of the factors which influence whether or not an operator will mention the risk associated with his job.

(*a*) Whether he has had, or seen an accident caused by this risk;

(*b*) how frequently such accidents occur;

(*c*) the seriousness of the resulting injury;

(*d*) the personal characteristics of the operator.

375 Of these, the first seems to be by far the most important; in other words operators learn to appreciate risks by profiting from their own mistakes and those of their neighbours. This reinforces the idea that training and safety propaganda must use situations familiar to the operator, and ones with which he can identify easily. These should preferably include incidents which have actually occurred in the particular factory concerned. It is no good at all showing an operator a page of statistics.

A. HALE

---

* The operators did not see these as risks because this was how it had always been. Some drills were never guarded, some covers were always off, some short cuts were the normal practice. – P.I.P.

Appendix 14
Subjective impressions of risk

376 An observer who had not previously been engaged in the accident study was taken round one of the sites and asked to say whether she considered the tasks she saw being performed to be relatively safe or to have some element of risk in them. She looked at 34 different tasks and rated 21 of them as being relatively safe and 13 as having a definite risk. This was done by looking for things about the task which she thought might cause an accident, such as sharp metal or glass edges, use of a power screwdriver, soldering iron, etc.

377 We then looked at the numbers of accidents on these tasks in relation to the number of times they were performed (this was done by comparing the number of accidents on each task with the number of times a second control was doing that task).

378 There were 306 accidents on the 13 'risky' tasks. From activity samples we found that second controls had done these tasks 212 times. There were 183 accidents on the 21 'safe' tasks, which the second controls had done 195 times. Relating accidents to the frequency with which the tasks were done gives a ratio of 1·43 accidents per task on the 'risky' tasks, and 0·93 accidents per task on the 'safe' tasks. (N.B. The frequencies here are only a sample whereas the accidents are totals on these tasks. Therefore, these figures do not give the true accident rates for the two categories of tasks.)

379 It appears that the observer was quite successful in picking out the tasks which were likely to cause accidents. However, looking at the figures for the individual tasks it appears that she misclassified some tasks as safe which did have a lot of accidents. An example of this is that she thought that packing the finished articles in cardboard boxes was safe, and did not notice the risk of cutting oneself on the sharp cardboard edges.

380 We also compared 13 people who had no accidents with 20 people who sustained more than six accidents, to see if the tasks they did most of the time (according to activity sample) fell into the 'risky' or the 'safe' category. The following results were obtained:

Table 16 – Accidents of people on 'safe' and on 'risky' jobs

	High accident people	Low accident people
Risky	15	3
Safe	5	10

High accident people did 'risky' tasks most of the time and low accident people did 'safe' tasks most of the time. This result was statistically significant (χ^2 test $p < 0.05$).

JEAN MARTIN
CAROLINE WARNE

Appendix 15
Major and minor accidents

Is there a statistical connection?
381 We found only 46 accidents at work which resulted in three or more days' lost time, compared with nearly 2,300 minor accidents; that is, about 2 out of every 100 injuries could be regarded as major.

382 The table in paragraph 120 of the report is based on the total figures, as follows:

Table 17 – Totals of all accidents

Department	Minor accident	Major accident	Period	Ratio: minor/major
Despatch	299	20	12 months	15
Rolling mill	391	9	12 months	43
Machine shop	808	15	21 months	54
Light assembly	823	2	21 months	412

383 The figures show a widely differing proportion of minor to major injury, and it is perhaps noteworthy that the lightest work produced the fewest major injuries. In the two shops at the top of the list, which both dealt with heavy work, the shop with least machinery, and therefore with most manual handling, produced the highest number of major injuries.

384 We were interested to see if individuals who sustained a higher-than-average number of minor accidents also had an unusual number of major accidents. Looking at the machine shop, we found that no-one had more than one major accident, and these are compared with total work accidents in the table overleaf:

Table 18 – Accidents of individuals and section average

Person's total work accidents	Average* total work accidents for the section where person worked
1	
6	} 6·0
19	
1	
1	
1	
3	} 5·5
4	
6	
3	1·2
6	4·6
1	
1	} 4·8
12	
2	0·9

* The averages were calculated for the people whe had been in the section for the whole period of the study.

385 Four of the people with a lower-than-average number of total work accidents left the workshop before the study was complete, and this could explain their low score. At the other end of the scale, two of the people with a higher-than-average number of total work accidents were outstanding cases of good operators, who worked fast on a variety of jobs, including special jobs and jobs new to the section. This probably explains their high score. So the table can be summarised thus:

Table 19 – Summary

Number of people	Relation to average number of work accidents	Probable reason
2	higher	Special work
4	higher	—
1	equal	—
4	lower	—
4	lower	Left before end of study period

386 This table suggests a fair distribution about the norm. We cannot go further without discussing individual cases, but there is no suggestion that major and minor accidents were statistically related in our machine shop.

387 The other department with a 'high' number of major accidents was the despatch. Here 15 of the major accidents were sustained by 13 people, who were all barrowmen. Two of these men were in the department for a short period only, and were excluded from analysis because their accident rates could not be calculated reliably. Using the Mann Whitney U-Test, we tested the difference between the accident rates of the remaining 11, and the accident rates of the other 33 barrowmen. We found that the men who had lost time accidents had significantly higher accident rates than the others in this group ($p = 0.0015$).

388 Of the other five lost time accidents at this department three were sustained by sorters and two by van-packers, but these numbers were not sufficient for statistical analysis.

389 Allowing for the relative population of sorters, barrowmen and van-packers, it appears that barrowmen had the job with the greatest risk of major accident. But we found that sorters sustained a significantly greater number of total accidents ($p = 0.05$).

Type and agent of injury
390 The differences between major and minor accidents stand out a little

Table 20 – Serious injuries in machine shop

Section	Agent of injury	Type of injury
Lathes	swarf	foreign body in eye
	swarf probably	foreign body in eye
	drill chip	foreign body in eye
Presses	*box*	cut finger
	floor	*bruised arm*
		strained shoulder
	truck handle	*crushed finger*
	press tool	*strained finger*
	press tool	*bruised abdomen and hernia*
	press guard	*bruised and cut head*
Gear-cutters	*rotary wire brush*	foreign body in eye
Drills	swarf	foreign body in eye
Grinders	bar material	*chipped bone of finger*
	floor	*broken bone on wrist*
	grinding wheel	*bruised* and cut finger
Inspection	*jig*	*bruised foot*

better when the type of injury and its agent are examined. Table 20 sets out these things for the major accidents in the machine shop. The italics indicate 'unusual'.

391 The most common minor injury in the machine shop was a small cut (mainly to the hand or fingers); over 60 per cent of the injuries were cuts. These were the result of contact with sharp edges on materials, components, machines and, to a lesser extent, various other minor causes, such as the boxes used to store components, and swarf. Yet a look at the injury column in the table above produces only three mentions of a cut, and two of these were associated with bruising by a violent impact.

392 The agents of major injury also tended to be uncommon, not so much on the lathes, where swarf accounted for well over a third of the total injuries, but in the other sections, with few exceptions. Even on the lathes, a piece of drill in the eye was a rare event (although it is a recognised source of serious injury).

393 Thus, on the presses, the press-tools caused few injuries, but three of them were serious. Boxes and truck-handles were also infrequent sources of minor injury. The floor seldom hurt anyone; people fell over on rare occasions!

394 In the gear-cutting section the rotary wire brush was an ancillary to the main work of cutting gears, and comparatively little was done with it. But it was an agent of major injury.

395 In the grinding section, contact with the grinding wheels occurred in only about six per cent of the total injuries.

396 The other shop with several major injuries was the despatch department. The analysis is shown opposite. As before, italics indicate 'unusual'.

397 The most common minor injury in the despatch department was also a cut to hand or finger: over 70 per cent of the injuries were of this type. Amongst the serious injuries, only two were cuts to the hand. Strains and severe bruising feature largely. The most common agents of minor injury were the metal corners of tea chests and the metal bands used to secure parcels. They featured in only three of the major injuries – the two cut hands mentioned above and a cut to the shoulder.

398 Thus the impression we have of the more serious injuries is that they tended to be the results of violent contact with unusual agents rather than more severe forms of the common injury.

399 This may be another way of saying that people have major accidents when faced with a hazard in an unusual form. In other words, this essay could be taken as another argument for better training and safeguarding.

Table 21 – Serious injuries in the despatch department

Agent of injury	Type of injury
Metal case	*strained back*
Barrow	*bruised ankle*
Tea chest	cut hand
Floor	*bruised hip and arm*
Cardboard carton	*strained back*
Side of van	*strained arm*
Barrow	*bruised ankle*
Wooden case	*bruised bone in foot*
Chain	*bruised head*
Side of van	*bruised ribs*
Barrow	*bruised leg*
Metal band	cut hand
Cardboard carton	*sprained wrist*
Floor	*sprained ankle*
Barrow	*twisted knee*
Tea chest	*bruised and cut shoulder*
Gap between van and platform	*bruised and cut knee*
Gap between van and platform	*fractured bone in foot and bruised knee*
Gap between van and platform	*damaged cartilage knee*
unknown	*rupture*

P. I. POWELL

M. SIMON

Appendix 16
By accident or design?

400 In this appendix, we tell the stories of some of the accidents we have seen during the study, together with a few of the more obvious ways of preventing such an accident in future. You will notice that we use the word 'obvious'. These things do seem fairly obvious once one has intimate knowledge of the circumstances surrounding the accident and it is for this reason that we advocate an accident prevention system which incorporates trainers who work in the shop for most of the time.

TWO CUTS FROM MATERIALS HANDLED

401 *First injury*. A man lifted a tea chest. A jagged edge of the corner reinforcement metal lacerated the side of his right hand. The injury required four stitches. The man was away from work for several days.

402 *Second injury*. In our goods despatch department, barrows like those used by porters on railway stations were often used to carry some of the larger parcels. One such parcel measured roughly 6 ft × 3 ft × 6 in. and was wrapped in stout brown paper secured by two metal bands. As you can perhaps imagine, this is an awkward size of parcel – it is as large as the mattress on a single bed. The man had to take this parcel through a doorway and this involved a certain amount of manoeuvring of the barrow and steadying of the load balanced on it. Having got the front of the barrow through the door, the man bumped his hand against the door jamb. His reflex action was to put his hand into contact with one of the metal bands around the parcel and he suffered an injury which required three stitches. He had to go home for a day or two.

403 Several **design** questions present themselves as a result of these two accidents:

(*a*) Tea chests are primarily for carrying tea, yet they are often used at second hand to carry a variety of other goods. They have been made in the same form since before the war, and if you like to ask which war, we think it must have been the Indian Mutiny. Their size is such that we found many of the men in the department experienced a certain amount of difficulty in grasping them. Their construction with thin sheet metal corner reinforcement, which usually comes away in various parts, and with nails which often stick out, is such that we found people handling them for any length of time had a relatively higher accident rate than with handling other types of package. In this age of plastics, it would not be expensive to mass-produce a non-injurious, conveniently-sized container which could be re-used many times.

(b) In the despatch department, handling a variety of goods day after day, parcels of the size of the one in the second accident came along fairly frequently. Here was a case for door-widening or, if that was structurally impracticable, the use of a form of barrow which cradled the load and allowed the man to use two hands to manoeuvre the barrow itself.

404 Training could affect the circumstances of these accidents in that the men could have been taught to work in gloves, and these might well have reduced the severity of the cuts, perhaps enabled the men to avoid them altogether. Of course, this implies the provision of suitable gloves and, as such, is really a matter of design of the job.

HOW INDUSTRY'S 'DONKEYS' CAN KICK

405 On three of our sites, fork lift trucks were used extensively. In one department, each driver normally worked on a particular truck. On the day of this accident, the driver was not operating his normal truck because this was being overhauled. After he had been using the truck allocated to him for a while, he had to adjust its forks to increase the distance between them for a new load. Both his usual truck and the allocated one had forks which ran along a horizontal slide.

406 On the driver's normal truck, the forks did not run very easily on the slide and so some force was needed to move them. He applied this same force to one of the forks on the strange truck. He pulled the fork right off the slide and it landed on his feet, giving him a severe injury which necessitated several days' absence.

407 This mishap could be **'designed** out':

(a) The best arrangement would probably be some form of screw-controlled slider, so that the driver could easily adjust the width between the forks by turning a handle. (It might even be a remote and power-operated control, so that the driver need not leave his seat.)

(b) Given that a driver does have to heave on a fork to shift it, some way of preventing the fork falling free must be provided. An end-stop on the slide in one way of doing this but some end-stops could make a nip for the fingers of the driver moving the fork. A chain of appropriate length between each fork and the centre of the slide could be used.

408 Training is secondary because the accident is positively prevented by end-stops. But encouragement to wear safety boots is always worth-while. So is instruction in where to place the hands on the forks, so that moving one up to an end-stop does not pinch a finger. (Might chains be better from this point of view?)

FOUR SLIPS ON A METAL SURFACE

409 In the despatch department, men often had to enter vans by metal bridge plates which spanned a gap of a few inches between the vans and the platform of the loading bay. The width of the plates was only a few inches wider than the track of the barrow wheels which the men used to carry heavy goods into the vans, and there was also a place either side of the plate where the gap was exposed. The floors of the vans were a few inches higher than the platform, and therefore the plates were at an angle.

410 *First injury.* A man pushing a loaded barrow up a metal bridge plate into a van, slipped on the plate and fell sideways and backwards. The barrow fell on his right leg, injuring it. He was absent for several weeks.

411 *Second injury.* The same kind of incident, but the man slipped and fell forwards against one side of the van, bruising his ribs. He was absent several days.

412 *Third injury.* A man carrying two cartons up a bridge plate into a van slipped on the plate, and fell forwards, injuring his elbow. He was absent for several weeks.

413 *Fourth injury.* One man went to the aid of another who was struggling to push a loaded barrow up a bridge plate. His foot slipped off the edge of the plate, into the gap between the van and the platform. He injured his knee, and was absent for several weeks. The plate was wet at the time because the roof leaked on to it.

414 **Design** is of paramount importance here.

(*a*) **Vans and platform of loading bay.**
    (i) Why not arrange the vans and platform to meet, so that the plates are unnecessary?

    (ii) Why not arrange the vans and platform at approximately the same height, so that the plates need not slope?

(*b*) **Alternatively (and very cheaply).**
    (i) Why not have bridge plates which span the gap between van and platform along the whole of the width of the van door?

    (ii) Why not rib the surface of the bridge plates, so that they are self-draining when wet and would in any event, provide a far better grip than does a smooth plate?

(c) **Footwear**
Why not provide vibram-soled boots? The cost of the absence of the men injured would more than pay for equipping the whole department.

(d) **Roof**
Surely the roof could be mended.

415 **Training** is secondary, but –

(a) Training was needed in the recognition of the size of load which can conveniently be handled in these awkward situations.

(b) Training is needed in the matter of wearing suitable boots, if they are provided.

CLOTHING RIPPED OFF WOMAN

416 A woman, drilling small components at a single-spindle bench drill, arranged the box of components to the left of the drill and the box of finished components to the right. She then reached across the front of the running drill with her right hand, to fetch a new component. Her sleeve caught on the drill and was wound onto it, but fortunately the drill chuck came away at its Morse taper fastening, and the woman's arm was only grazed. *but arm badly cut*

417 This is potentially a very serious accident. It raises questions of **design**:

(a) Why was the drill unguarded? It is certainly a dangerous part of the machine, as the events proved, and it requires secure fencing in accordance with Section 14 of the Factories Act 1961. The usual legal interpretation of 'secure fencing' is 'a fence which will positively prevent the operator coming into contact with the dangerous part'. On this particular job the use of secure fencing would probably have involved a mechanical sliding feed arrangement to take each component up to the drilling point. This is such a common safety need that we wonder why drill manufacturers are not persuaded to make slides on their drill tables as a standard fitting.

(b) Her sleeve was an overall sleeve – the garment being provided by the firm. It is commonly accepted that lathe operators work sleeveless, so why not drill operators? (This might have been an administrative slip, but neither the foreman nor the setter noticed it, until it was too late.)

418 And questions of **training**:

(a) The operator could have been taught about the need to stay sleeveless.

(b) She could have been taught the appropriate hand movements, viz, 'pick up with your left; discard with your right,' etc.

NEAR DISASTER WHILST SETTING A POWER-PRESS

419 In a press shop, there were some single-stroke power presses and some automatic presses which were fed with strip. These latter were used to make washers and similar small parts by the several thousand.

420 One fitter had a group of the single-stroke presses in his charge. He was a competent man and seldom kept people waiting for work. When he set a machine, he would isolate its electric motor. If he wanted to move the mechanism, he would bar the flywheel, which had holes in its periphery for this purpose. He was accustomed to testing the scrap ejector of a top tool by turning over the press with the bar in his right hand and catching in his left hand the scrap as it dropped from the top tool, i.e. his hand would be between the press tools.

421 One day, a colleague was away from the group of automatic presses. Our fitter was transferred to them. The flywheel was inaccessible and could not be turned by hand but there were two 'inch' buttons, one marked 'forward' and the other 'reverse'. So our fitter did his final adjustments with the motor energised and he made small movements of the mechanism by using the 'inch' buttons.

422 As was his habit, he put his left hand under the top tool to catch a sample of product and 'inched' the machine. Either he pressed the 'forward' button when the tool was already on the down-stroke or the 'reverse' button when the tool was still on the upstroke, for the top tool, instead of moving upwards, closed towards the bottom tool and trapped the setter's left hand. Fortunately, because the 'inch' mechanism gave only a limited movement to the machine, the top tool did not close completely on to the lower tool. The setter's fingers were held and pierced in places by locating pins but the injuries were comparatively minor and he was absent from work for only a few hours.

423 He told our observer what a dilemma he was in when trapped. He knew that he was not seriously injured but that to release his hand without turning the mechanism would be a lot of work for a fitter. He could release himself simply by pressing the 'inch' button to raise the top tool, but *which* 'inch' button? He did not know if he had advanced the machine on to his hand or reversed it. He could not see the crankshaft of the machine, to identify the position in the cycle. If he pressed the wrong button now, he would lose his hand.

424 He eventually decided that the top tool must have been on the upstroke because he had been waiting for the scrap to eject and this happens as the top tool reaches the top of its stroke. So his mistake must have been to press the reverse 'inch' button rather than the 'forward' one. He bravely pressed the 'forward' inch button and proved himself correct. I think I would rather have had fitters dismantle the machine.

425 This raises several questions of **design**:

(*a*) Why was the automatic machine designed with two similar 'inch' buttons, side by side?

(*b*) Why not make one button 'feel' different? e.g., a hinged flap normally kept in position over it by gravity or a rough surface to it or an unusual shape, or all three.

(*c*) Why not duplex buttons, so that two hands are necessary on the buttons?

(*d*) Why not an interlocked guard to the dangerous parts, so that *no* powered motion of the press is possible with hands near the tools?

After the accident, the firm concerned adopted remedy (*d*).

426 And two matters of **training**:

(*a*) Our setter had a bad habit of putting his left hand between press tools when it was not strictly necessary. Even on his own machines, he could have made some error of judgment and pulled the press tool down on to his own hand.

(*b*) He did not realise that methods he could use with only small risk on his own machines would involve large risk on the automatic machines. He had not been trained to regard setting of an energised machine as especially hazardous.

P. I. POWELL
M. SIMON
M. HALE

Appendix 17
Ergonomics of goods handling

427 The Department of Engineering Production at Birmingham University was invited by the National Institute of Industrial Psychology to carry out a short ergonomic study of the manual and mechanical handling used in the despatch department, and to suggest possible improvements, with particular reference to the accidents which had been observed. The following summarises the full report (by R. E. Stockbridge).

428 The report draws attention to such things as uneven and obstructed floors; vans with low roofs and poorly illuminated; a leaking departmental roof; cranes with mechanisms too easily started unintentionally; the variety of widths of loading gangways into vans; the small use of protective clothing, particularly gloves; the lack of a training programme; poor work methods. On the basis of these observations a number of recommendations are made.

Increased mechanisation (in the long term)
429 Mechanisation of the department as a whole to a much greater extent, as we saw in another despatch department we visited during the study.

Improved packaging of goods
430 Handles or slots on packages to facilitate handling.

431 Plastic bands to fasten packages in preference to metal bands. Metal bands were the agent of injury in approximately 25 per cent of the accidents involving packages. This includes nine severe injuries.

432 The use of tea chests to be discontinued, or the senders instructed to keep them in good repair. Tea chests were the agent of injury in approximately 29 per cent of the accidents involving packages. This includes ten more severe injuries.

Improved mechanical equipment
433 Span plates to be a standard width of not less than 48 in., and made of a light alloy to reduce weight and facilitate handling (also ribbed to offer a safer foothold). Six of the more severe injuries occurred when men slipped on, or missed completely, the metal span plates which bridged a gap between lorries and work platform.

434 Portable conveyor to go inside the lorries to aid unloading. Suitable auxiliary equipment would reduce the physical strain of manual handling. Four more severe strain injuries occurred after men had handled heavy or awkwardly-sized goods in the confined space of the lorries.

435 Regular maintenance of all equipment, e.g., barrows, would forestall many of the complaints about the condition of equipment. Lack of maintenance of much of the equipment appeared to contribute to increased effort and therefore unnecessary fatigue.

Improved physical environment
436 Correction of defects in the physical environment, e.g., floor surface, roof leakage. Two more severe injuries and countless other incidents were contributed to by unsatisfactory floor surfaces. One of these was after roof leakage had made the surface dangerously slippery.

437 Two white parallel lines to clearly mark gangways. Two more severe injuries occurred after collisions between two men manoeuvring their loads in congested 'gangway' space, and several minor collisions were observed.

438 Encouragement of men to keep gangways free of obstruction. This would be helped by good supervisor training. See para. 437 examples above, plus many minor bumps and knocks with goods piled in congested 'gangways'.

439 Obsolete weighing scales and five of the fixed cranes could be removed, which would increase working space. Alternatively, all the fixed cranes could be removed and replaced by a travelling hoist. One more severe injury occurred when a fixed crane which was never used was inadvertently set in motion.

Protective equipment
440 Appropriate protective clothing, e.g., gloves, to be supplied to the workmen. Over 70 per cent of the injuries observed might have been prevented if suitably designed clothing had been worn.

Training
441 Formal training in safe methods of lifting and handling for new recruits either by:

(*a*) attendance at one of the existing courses on handling methods,
or
(*b*) instruction from a gang specially chosen for the correct handling methods, good discipline and clear communications of its members, who must be trained in methods of instruction.

442 Safety training was negligible, yet it might have prevented several injuries, e.g., five more severe injuries occurred when goods were badly loaded on to barrows. In three cases the load was top-heavy and overbalanced on to the man. In the other two, the load was insecure and part toppled on to a man. All five cases involved fundamental errors of loading. Many more incidents of these types were observed. Most of the men were observed using dangerous methods of handling. Although four more severe strain injuries that occurred were contributed to by other factors (see para. 434), another occurred despite a man having plenty of space to lift safely.

Responsibility for safety
443 Safety to be the specific responsibility of one of the supervisors (this department did not have a resident safety officer).

JAYNE DAVIES
M. SIMON

Appendix 18
Monthly distribution of accidents

444 The numbers of accidents per calendar month, standardised to a base of 20 working days per month, are shown in Figures 3–6 for the four shops. Cross comparisons of the numbers of accidents represented are not valid, because the populations are different.

445 The fluctuations at the machine and assembly shops can be explained largely in terms of recruitment (see Appendix para. 342). We thought that the changing work load probably also affected the distributions, but the work was so varied and complex that we found this impossible to measure and test (see Appendix para. 307).

Monthly accident distribution (based on 20 days per month)

Figure 3   Machine shop

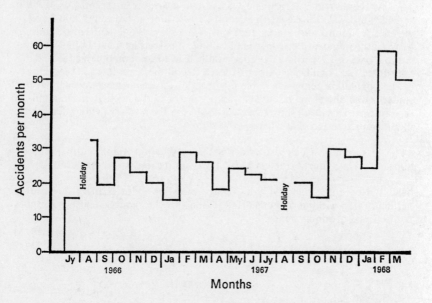

Monthly accident distribution (based on 20 days per month)
Figure 4   Assembly shop

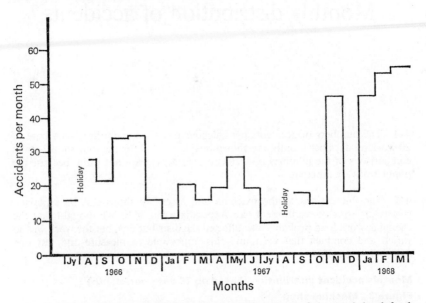

446 At the despatch department we had two measures of the work load, both of which showed the seasonal variations. For example, December and January were slack months and March and April were busy. We tested the relationship between the number of accidents and volume of parcels handled, both standardised to a base of 20 working days per month. The correlation obtained (Kendall's tau $=0.462$) was significant at the 0.02 level. Recruitment was low and the majority of the population remained stable members of the department throughout our study. It was, therefore, not a contributory factor to the fluctuations in numbers of accidents. This result shows that work load was the primary factor affecting the monthly distribution of accidents at this shop.

447 At the mill, which also had a stable population, the monthly variation appeared to be a function of work load and overtime (see Appendix para. 644).

448 We conclude that it is unwise to generalise about changes in monthly accident rates, without first exploring reasons for the changes. This also applies to discussion of annual trends.

JEAN MARTIN
M. SIMON

Monthly accident distribution (based on 20 days per month)
Figure 5 Despatch department

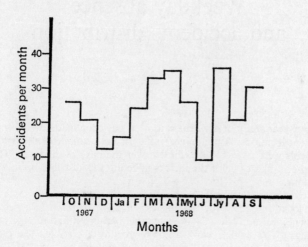

Figure 6 Mill

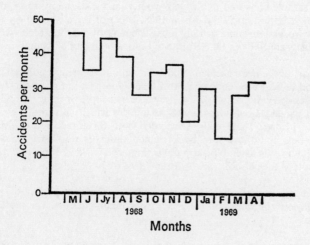

Appendix 19
Weekday absence
and accidents distribution

449 A four-year study of accident causation has been made by the Institute at four different locations. A preliminary analysis on a sample of the data showed that accidents were unevenly distributed over the days of the week. This paper takes a closer look at one of the factors affecting this distribution in one of the four locations.

450 The location chosen for the purpose of this paper was an assembly shop in a light engineering factory. It was suitable because it had a large number of women engaged in similar work and was readily accessible. The other three locations included in the main study were less suitable for a variety of reasons e.g. shift work, smaller sample size, inaccessibility.

451 The sample consisted of the 197 women in the assembly shop who were still employed by the firm on 5 April, 1968. Most of these worked on assembly lines; a few worked on sub-assembly jobs. The majority of the women were Irish, and their ages ranged from 18–60 (mean age 34). About half of them were married.

452 As part of the main accident study, data about accidents had been collected for a period of 88 weeks ending in April 1968. Information was collected about injuries sustained at home, work and elsewhere by people working in this location, but in this paper we consider only those injuries which occurred at work from Monday to Friday. These injuries included both those reported to the factory medical centre and those seen by a trained observer who spent most of the working day in this assembly shop collecting accident and supplementary data for the whole of the period.

453 There are several factors which influence the distribution of accidents over the days of the week and these factors probably interact. The most obvious factors are:

(*a*) If a woman is away from work she cannot have an accident, so we needed to know the number of people in our sample who were at work on each of the five days. Similarly no-one in the department (except the maintenance men) could have accidents on public holidays.

(Reproduced from NIIP Bulletin, Summer 1970)

(b) If a woman works twice as fast on one day as on the next, she will come into contact with twice as many components, and it can be argued that her risk of injury by components is greater on the first day. If more work is consistently done on one weekday rather than another, it is likely to be reflected in different accident rates on different days (and in this location this factor is relevant).

(c) Some jobs incur more risk than others. If such jobs are performed more on one day than another, a higher accident rate on that day would be likely.

(d) If overtime is consistently done on some days rather than others (this is very usual in industry generally), people are at work and exposed to the risk of injury for more hours on these days and so more accidents could be expected on these days of the week.

454 This paper is concerned with the first of these factors. This factor is basic, as a correction must be made for the numbers of days worked before considering any of the other factors.

455 Details of absence for the women in the sample were collected from the personnel department. A previous study had compared the personnel department records with the computer print-out from the wages department and had found the personnel records to be an accurate source of absence data. The company coded the data on special cards, one card per person per year. The cards for 1967 and 1968 were kept in special files and updated daily. Cards for earlier years were kept with each individual's personal dossier. When someone left, his absence data were summarised on a leaver's card and the original records destroyed. Our absence data were collected after the 88 weeks' accident observation and we could not obtain absence information for women who had left the employment of the firm before 5 April 1968.

456 The absence data obtained from personnel records included sickness, permitted unpaid leave, absence without permission and long term service bonus days. From this we found the total numbers of absences for the five different days of the week.

457 In order to find the numbers of each day of the week that were actually worked, it was also necessary to take into account public and union-agreed holidays. The 88-week period included two summer holidays, each of a fortnight. These do not affect the distribution because everyone was away from work for four of each of the weekdays.

458 Ninety-nine women were employed for all 88 weeks and each missed the same number of public and union holidays i.e., nine Mondays, two Tuesdays and three Fridays. For the remaining 98 individuals, corrections had to be made for the numbers of public and union holidays each person had missed. This correction depended on each individual's starting date and a further correction was necessary, because individuals started work on different days of the week. On the basis of these corrections, it was possible to calculate the numbers of each day of the week which were available to be worked by the people in our sample. These were as follows:

Total number of woman-days available

Monday	Tuesday	Wednesday	Thursday	Friday	Total
10,623	11,451	11,735	11,739	11,388	56,936

459 The total number of each of the five weekdays missed through the various causes of absence (see above) was subtracted from the number of the available weekdays. This gave the total number of each weekday that was actually worked.

Total number of days absence

Monday	Tuesday	Wednesday	Thursday	Friday	Total
1,311	1,085	1,040	960	1,246	5,642

Total number of woman-days actually worked

Monday	Tuesday	Wednesday	Thursday	Friday	Total
9,312	10,366	10,695	10,779	10,142	51,294

460 The figures for the numbers of accidents occurring on the different days of the week were as follows:

Monday	Tuesday	Wednesday	Thursday	Friday	Total
91	82	102	68	63	406

461 From these, it appears that the highest number of accidents occurred on Wednesday and the least on Friday. However, these figures do not give a true picture, because the same numbers of Wednesdays and Fridays were not worked.

462 To correct for the different number of days worked and to enable comparisons to be made, a standard rate can be used. A standard accident rate could be expressed as the number of accidents per 100 man days worked:

$$\text{Rate} = \frac{\text{actual number of accidents}}{\text{actual number of man-days worked}} \times 100$$

463 This gives the following figures for our sample:

Monday	Tuesday	Wednesday	Thursday	Friday
0·98	0·79	0·96	0·63	0·62

Similarly an overall accident rate can be calculated; in this case, it is 0·79 per cent.

464 The advantage of this method is that the rates are independent of the number of people in the sample and the number of days worked, and give manageable figures with this kind of data.

465 A limitation is that the rate does not take into account any variation in the hours worked on the various weekdays. To allow for such variations, e.g., overtime, the accident rate needs to be in terms of the number of accidents for a standard number of hours worked. However, in the assembly shop from which our data came, a negligible amount of weekday overtime was worked and so in this particular case, the rates calculated give a true picture.

Summary
466 The totals of accidents occurring on different days of the week do not give a true picture of accident distribution over the week, because different numbers of the five weekdays will have been worked. The greater the difference between the number of days worked, the less meaningful the accident totals are.

467 The standard accident rate calculated as shown, corrects for this. The rate is useful for comparing data from different places, or for different groups of people; but the records from which the data are collected must be comparable in the first place.

JEAN MARTIN
CAROLINE WARNE

Appendix 20
Distribution of accidents
over the days of the week

468 The numbers of accidents occurring on each weekday at our four shops are shown in the following table. The numbers are expressed as rates, which take into account the number of man days actually worked on each day of the week (see the previous Appendix).

Table 22 – Accident rates over the days of the week

	Mon	Tue	Wed	Thur	Fri
Assembly women	0·98	0·79	0·96	0·63	0·62
Machine men	1·23	1·07	1·08	1·10	0·93
Machine women	0·97	0·73	0·86	1·03	0·92
Despatch department					
Early shift	2·10	1·81	1·78	1·79	1·86
Late shift	1·24	1·42	1·23	2·08	1·45
Mill	1·96	1·78	1·85	1·93	1·60

469 Two major factors appeared to affect the distribution of accidents over the days of the week. These were the work load and absence.

Work load
470 We found it impractical to measure work load at the assembly and machine shops because the work involved a large range of machines and components. The variations between jobs in both shops were such that straight measures of output would not reflect the content of the work done. However, people told us that they did less work on Thursdays (pay-day) and Fridays (start of the weekend) and this probably explains the lower accident rates on Thursday and Friday for women in the assembly shop, and Friday for men in the machine shop.

471 At the mill, we observed that people were busy for the first four days of the week and only relaxed a little on Friday, which was pay-day. Friday was the lowest accident day at this shop.

472 At the despatch department, the accident rate remained roughly constant for each shift, apart from the Monday early shift and the Thursday late shift. We thought the higher rate for the Monday early shift was probably the effect of absence (see para. 478, later). The Thursday late shift was a particularly busy period, because it was the last time in which packing could be completed for delivery the same week.

473 All the men handled goods, so, as suggested at paragraph 327 the volume handled would have been a meaningful measure of work done. We would have expected this to correlate with accidents per day. Unfortunately, we did not gather data for volume per day, because several vans were left partly filled overnight and the estimation of volume every night was too time consuming for us.

474 We could find the weight handled per day from the firm's records and the averages of these, over the year, are:

Monday	...	...	...	...	...	...	...	358·6 tons
Tuesday	...	...	...	...	...	...	...	345·6 tons
Wednesday	...	...	...	...	...	...	...	347·6 tons
Thursday	...	...	...	...	...	...	...	350·3 tons
Friday	...	...	...	...	...	...	...	345·8 tons

The Monday and Thursday weights are in fact the largest but we found there was no statistical relationship between weights and the pattern of accidents (similar in paragraph 321). The small variation in the weights is really a comment on the system of bonus calculation at the department. Bonus was paid on weight per day and each day was a fresh start.

Absence
475 Absence was highest on Mondays (apart from the machine shop men) and lowest on pay-days, with intermediate days graduated between these extremes. This is illustrated in the table below; figures for pay-days are in bold print.

Table 23 – Percentage of man days lost through absence

	Mon	Tue	Wed	Thur	Fri
Assembly women	12·3	9·5	8·9	**8·2**	10·9
Machine men	8·4	8·2	7·3	**6·4**	8·6
Machine women	9·8	9·3	8·6	**8·3**	9·1
Despatch department	15·5	14·3	14·5	14·3	**14·1**
Mill	12·9	12·2	12·3	12·2	**11·5**

476 The pattern of this table stands out if rank orders are considered, as shown overleaf. The number 1 stands for the highest absence of the week.

477 On Monday, when absence was high, more than usual of those who came to work had to tackle an unfamiliar task in order that the more essential work was done. We tested this in the assembly and machine shops by analysing the 'done before' measure of experience on a specific task (see Appendix paras.

344–348). We calculated the percentage of accidents on each day of the week where the first control had done the task never, rarely or occasionally.

Table 24 – Rank order of absence through the week

	Mon	Tue	Wed	Thur	Fri
Assembly women	1	3	4	5	2
Machine men	2	3	4	5	1
Machine women	1	2	4	5	3
Despatch department	1	3½	2	3½	5
Mill	1	3½	2	3½	5

Table 25 – Number of accidents recorded and task experience of first controls on different days of the week

	Mon	Tue	Wed	Thur	Fri
Number of accidents (not corrected for absence)	77	78	89	72	65
Percentage of accidents where first control had done the task never, rarely or occasionally	20·8%	15·4%	15·7%	9·7%	18·5%

478 The pattern of the percentage of accidents where the first control had done the task never, rarely or occasionally is similar to the pattern of absence for the different days of the week, with high absence on Mondays and Fridays and low absence on Thursdays. The figures confirmed our view that people more often do unfamiliar tasks when there is a lot of absence.

479 We found that people are more likely to have accidents on unfamiliar tasks. The task experience of victims fell significantly more often into one of the three short experience categories of never, rarely and occasionally than into the three longer experience categories.

480 Therefore, in situations where tasks have to be rearranged among people because of absence, absence will influence the distribution of accidents.

481 At the despatch department, the work was very similar and all the men were concerned in the handling of goods. There were, however, some differences between the three occupational categories of sorters, van packers and barrowmen. When men were absent the groups obviously had to be reorganised. This often resulted in a barrowman sorting for a day. We counted the number of occasions when this occurred, and found it most frequent on Mondays, as would be expected from the higher absence on that day.

The number of occasions on which barrowmen sorted because of sorters' absence was:

Monday	...	...	...	...	...	...	...	43
Tuesday	...	...	...	...	...	...	...	23
Wednesday	...	...	...	...	...	...	...	20
Thursday	...	...	...	...	...	...	...	13
Friday	...	...	...	...	...	...	...	16

482 There was most absence from the Monday early shift, when nearly 17 per cent of man days were lost through this cause. On this particular shift, more people were doing unfamiliar work and working in unfamiliar groups, because of the reorganisation necessitated by absence, than on any other shift during the week. We think that this situation contributed to the high accident rate for that shift.

JEAN MARTIN
M. SIMON

Appendix 21
Distribution of accidents over hours of the day in all four shops

Assembly and machine shops

483 Histograms (Figures 7–9) illustrate the accident distribution in half-hour periods over the day in the assembly and machine shops. There was an official tea break in the morning from 09.50 until 10.00, lunch was from 12.00 until 12.45, and people also took an unofficial break in the afternoon around 14.30.

484 The histograms* show that there were more accidents in the morning than the afternoon, that the peak time for accidents occurred after mid-morning, and that there tended to be peaks in the accident distribution just before the breaks.

Distribution of accidents in half-hour periods over the day

Figure 7 Assembly shop (paced and unpaced)

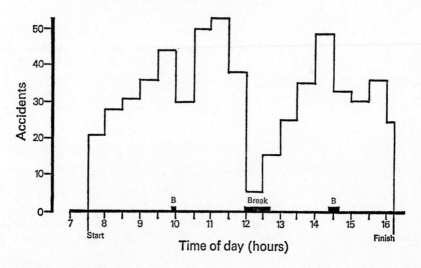

* Cross comparisons of the numbers of accidents in figures 7 to 16 are not valid because the populations differ.

Figure 8 Machine shop (unpaced work)

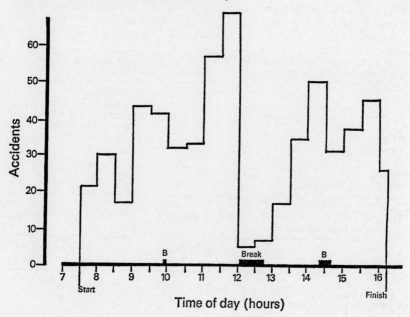

Figure 9 Assembly shop (paced only)

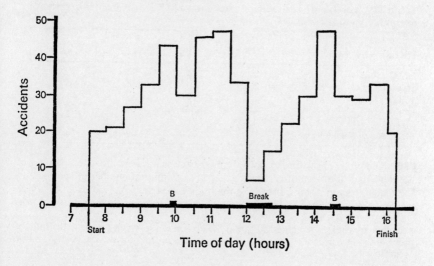

485 We therefore looked more closely at the accidents which occurred in the three or four half-hours before each break for the men and women in the machine shop, and the women in the assembly shop. The results are shown in the following three tables.†

Table 26 – Number of accidents in successive half-hours before breaks for machine shop men

| Period of day | Time before break | | | |
	2 to 1½ hrs.	1½ to 1 hr.	1 to ½ hr.	Last ½ hr.
07.50 – 09.50	23	15	31	25
10.00 – 12.00	26	26	36	45
13.00 – 14.30	—	14	24	31
14.40 – 16.10	—	27	26	30
TOTAL	49	82	117	131
Mean accidents per hour	49	41	59	66

Table 27 – Number of accidents in successive half-hours before breaks for machine shop women

| Period of day | Time before break | | | |
	2 to 1½ hrs.	1½ to 1 hr.	1 to ½ hr.	Last ½ hr.
07.50 – 09.50	9	4	10	17
10.00 – 12.00	6	7	21	23
13.00 – 14.30	—	2	10	18
14.40 – 16.10	—	9	7	15
TOTAL	15	22	48	73
Mean accidents per hour	15	11	24	37

Table 28 – Number of accidents in successive half-hours before breaks for assembly shop women

| Period of day | Time before break | | | |
	2 to 1½ hrs.	1½ to 1 hr.	1 to ½ hr.	Last ½ hr.
07.50 – 09.50	24	24	34	38
10.00 – 12.00	23	40	44	34
13.00 – 14.30	—	21	32	41
14.40 – 16.10	—	35	23	32
TOTAL	47	120	133	145
Mean accidents per hour	47	60	67	73

486 The tables show that in both shops there was a rise in the mean number of accidents per hour as a break approached. The minimum number of accidents in the machine shop occurred towards the middle of a work period (each of which was roughly two hours). This seems to be the time after initial settling down,

† In this appendix, the figures are for those accidents for which we knew the time of occurrence. Hence, a number of accidents are excluded because we did not know accurately the time of occurrence.

and the time before aiming at a target as the next break looms ahead.

487 The speed of working of the women on the assembly lines was paced by the moving conveyor belt.* Most operators in the machine shop had full control over their speed of working. We thought that the accident distribution over the day was partly determined by the speed of work. If this were so, there would be a difference in the accident distribution between paced and unpaced work. All the people in the machine shop were doing unpaced work, and Figure 8 shows this distribution. Figure 9 shows the accident distribution for the women who did paced work on the assembly lines in the assembly shop.

488 The peaks in the accident distribution for the unpaced work are more marked than those for the paced work. This appears to be mainly the effect of the target-setting by operators whose work was individual. They tended to start work slowly and then increase their speed of working towards a break to achieve their target.

489 As part of other research in progress in the factory, the electricity consumption of the machine shop (and another small shop which we were not studying) was measured at three-minute intervals over one day. We examined the distribution obtained in relation to the accident distribution for the machine shop over the whole of our study period. The electricity readings were averaged over half-hour periods corresponding to the half-hour periods of the accident distribution. The table below shows the distributions of accidents and electricity consumption.

Table 29 – Accidents and electricity consumption

Time	Number of accidents in machine shop	Average electricity consumption
10.00 – 10.30	32	221 amps
10.30 – 11.00	33	223
11.00 – 11.30	57	239
11.30 – 12.00	68	231
13.30 – 14.00	34	197
14.00 – 14.30	49	205
14.30 – 15.00	31	199
15.00 – 15.30	39	206
15.30 – 16.00	49	212

490 We calculated Spearman's Rank Correlation Co-efficient on these figures and obtained a value for rho of 0·58. The value required for statistical significance at the 5 per cent level of probability is 0·60, and so this result is almost significant. However, the electricity consumption was measured on one day only; did not start until 10.00 hours; and the measure included another shop whose accidents we were not investigating.

* i.e. Members of each team had only limited control over their speed of working (the supervisor could alter the belt speed, on request).

124   2000 ACCIDENTS

The despatch department
491 This department had an early shift (08.00 – 17.00 hrs) and a late (11.00 – 20.00 hrs) one. The men alternated weekly between them. The time distribution of accidents is shown by the histograms (Figures 10–11). The shifts are treated separately, as the factors which contributed to accidents varied in degree between them.

Distribution of accidents over the day in half hour periods
Figure 10   Despatch department (early shift)

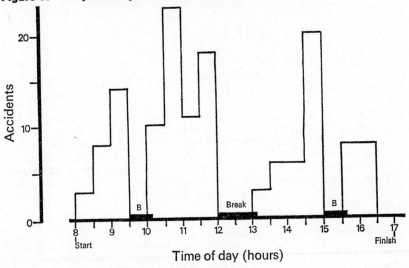

Figure 11   Despatch department (late shift)

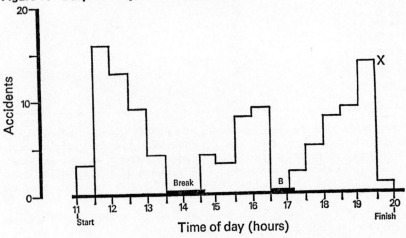

492 At this shop, we found relationships between some measures of work and accidents (see Appendix para. 327), i.e., the more goods a man handled the greater his exposure to risk and therefore accident. The distribution of accidents during the day may be related to the variation in exposure to risk caused by the different times that lorries entered the shop for unloading, and the consequent changes in the availability of work. Some periods of the day were busier than others and we would expect more accidents during these periods. Lorries were brought into the department when the drivers had completed a particular round. This occurred spasmodically during most of the day until approximately 17.30 hrs when all the drivers started to bring in their lorries. The busiest periods of the day were therefore from 17.30 hrs onwards and in the mornings. The direct results of the time organisation of the drivers' work is discussed below.

Early shift

493 Usually, the men on the early shift were busy from the beginning of the shift. The busy period sometimes extended to the lunch break at 12.00 hrs. Initially, the men unloaded, sorted and re-loaded the goods in lorries left from the end of their shift the previous day. Their work places were often full in the morning because more lorries arrived in the evening period than the late shift could clear, and those over were put in the early shift's work places. This probably explains the higher number of accidents occurring in the mornings than the afternoons.

494 Contributing to the lower number of accidents during the periods 08.00 to 08.30, 10.00 to 10.30, 11.00 to 11.30 hrs were:

(a) shortened periods of work; the men did not often start work before 08.15 hrs. and the breakfast break usually extended to 10.10 hrs. Thus, two half-hour periods were decreased by almost half for much of the time.

(b) the late shift started work at about 11.10 to 11.15 hrs and the resulting confusion, while people hailed each other and found their barrows, affected the amount of work done by the early shift during that half-hour period.

495 The afternoons were usually fairly slack. The late shift had lunch break from 13.30 to about 14.40 hrs and, during that time, any lorries that came into the department tended to be put in the early shift's work places. If lorries did arrive, the early shift had a slightly busier period from 14.00 to 15.00 hrs than they had from 13.00 to 14.00 hrs. This may have contributed to the peak of accidents from 14.30 to 15.00 hrs. We think the lack of a peak between 16.00 and 16.30 hours is explained by the work having eased off towards the end of the early shift. It was established shop practice that the men would stop work around 16.30 hrs so that they could wash and change before leaving. No accidents were recorded after 16.30 hrs on the early shift, and this was because very little work was done after this time.

Late shift

496 The late shift had busy periods at the beginning and end of each day.

As most lorries entered the department after 17.30 hrs, the period 18.00 to 18.30 hrs was usually their busiest time.

497   The bonus system was such that, after a certain tonnage had been cleared, the bonus rate increased for each extra ton handled. There was a tendency to 'rush' towards the end of the day in order to finish loads and achieve this higher bonus rate, because the weights of finished loads were included in the total of tonnage handled for that day, and unfinished loads would otherwise be carried over to the next day at the lower rate. The rush to finish loads may explain the 19.00 to 19.30 hrs peak of accidents. It was established shop practice that the men would stop work around 19.30 hrs on this shift, and only one accident was recorded after this time.

498   Too many lorries came in during the evening period for the late shift to unload. Inevitably, several were left in the late shift's work places and, consequently, they were busy in the morning. The initial busy period from 11.15 hours onwards may explain the high numbers of accidents from 11.30 to 12.30 hrs. The afternoon periods were slack up to about 18.00 hrs.

499   The peaked time distribution of accidents at the despatch department is therefore largely explained in terms of availability of work and hours of work.

Distribution of accidents over the day in half-hour periods
Rolling mill
Figure 12   Day shift

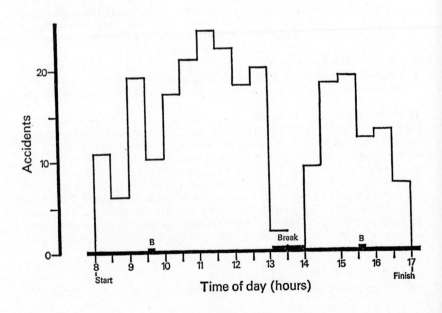

Rolling mill
500 The three histograms (Figures 12, 13 and 14) illustrate the accident distribution in half-hour periods over the day for the three shifts. The lunch and tea breaks for the different shifts are shown.

Figure 13   Morning shift

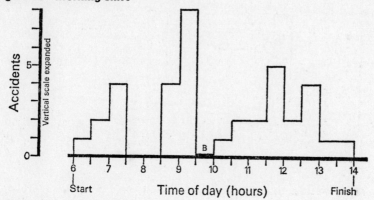

Figure 14   Afternoon shift

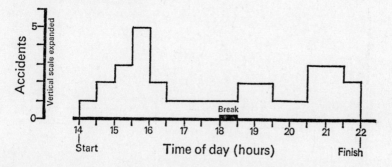

501 Relatively few accidents were observed on the morning and afternoon shifts, and therefore we cannot really comment on their distribution.

502 The histogram for the day shift (Figure 12) shows that more accidents occurred in the morning than in the afternoon. There are peaks in the distribution before each of the three breaks, and the accidents tail off towards the end of the day. However, there is also a peak of accidents in the middle of the morning, around 11.00 hrs. The observer at this site formed a subjective impression of a build-up of work at about this time, which might be an explanation of this peak.

503 To try to confirm this impression, we looked at the time distribution of accidents that occurred when people said they were working faster than normal, and when they were working at normal speed. Figures 15 and 16 show the

Distribution of accidents over the day in half-hour periods
Rolling mill
Figure 15 Pattern of accidents of people who said they were working faster than usual

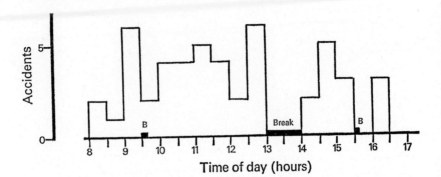

Figure 16 Pattern of accidents of people who said they were working at usual speed

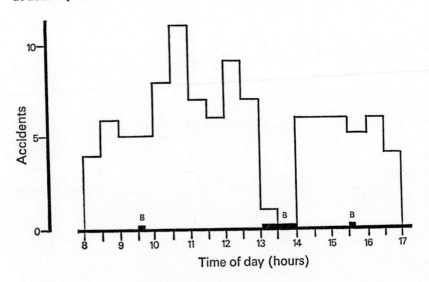

distributions obtained. We did not have complete information on how fast people were working, so the number of accidents shown in these two histograms is not equal to the total number shown in Figures 12, 13 and 14. The histogram for accidents which occurred when people were working faster than normal shows very marked peaks before the morning breaks, whereas these are not so apparent when people were working at normal speed. Both histograms show a mid-morning peak when there was the highest pressure of work.

JEAN MARTIN
MARY HALE
M. SIMON

Appendix 22
A field study of repetitive manual work in relation to accidents at the work place

504 The author of this article, Paul Branton, carried out the field work described whilst he was a member of the External Scientific Staff of the Medical Research Council attached to the NIIP Accident Research Team. He provided us with a copy of the article and it also appeared in the International Journal of Production Research (1970) Volume 8, Number 2, published by the Institution of Production Engineers, 10 Chesterfield Street, London W1. Paul Branton is now Ergonomist, British Railways Board, London NW1.

SUMMARY

505 Four hundred and twenty-seven reported accidents in the course of repetitive, self-paced work in the machine shop of a light engineering factory were analysed for time of occurrence. Four critical peak periods were found. During these periods observational studies of variability of speed of operation were conducted, particularly on lathes, which revealed that machine loading times varied more than cutting times. This was followed by a case study of variability of accuracy of hand movements. Unsuccessful Hand Movements (UHM's) were found to occur more often during the critical periods than at other times of the day. The data are interpreted in terms of rate of gain of information, fatigue and boredom.

INTRODUCTION

506 In a discussion of conceptual models in accident research, McFarland (1963) considered an accident as 'the end product of a sequence of acts or events which results in some "unanticipated" consequence judged as "undesirable" '. The aim of accident research – and prevention – is thus to foresee the unanticipated. This formulation presents in a nutshell the circular problem in defining accidents and directs attention to the difficulty of establishing the *antecedents* to accidental injury from *post hoc* records. In the present state of knowledge about accident causation this is inevitable. It may nevertheless be possible to extract useful material from records gathered after the event and to follow up the proposal made by Suchman (1961) that a class of events be studied quite independently of their consequences, i.e. presence or absence of injury. This paper describes the attempt of selecting a class of events from among which accidental injury at the work place might possibly be expected. It also attempts to relate to the workshop situation concepts used in the laboratory study of human performance.

507 It takes its starting points from two recent field research findings: more accidents occur at certain times of the working day than at others; hand injuries made up over 70 per cent of all accidents reported. That field work, conducted by a team from the National Institute of Industrial Psychology, was a two-year study of accidents in the machine and assembly shops of a large light engineering factory, and the present study refers to a group of operatives in the same workshop and to the same conditions.

The findings of the NIIP team on the temporal distribution of accidents over the working day will be considered first.

Peak times of accident occurrence

508 The main point of technique here is that the NIIP team had manned the workshop continuously throughout the working days of two years. From the resulting records of over 2,000 accidents, the present author selected 427 cases by the following criteria:

(a) they occurred at the actual *work station* and during normal work operations;

(b) *nature* and *locus* of injury, and *time* of occurrence were known;

(c) the *machine* at which the accident happened and the *job description* (in work study terms) were available.

These 427 recorded accidents involved 141 operatives, out of a total of about 180, accidents per operative ranging from one (N=59) to seventeen (N=3). The distribution of reported times of occurrence is shown as a histogram in Figure 17. The data are grouped into 15 min. intervals, this being the shortest interval warranted without exaggerating accuracy of reporting. As a further precaution against too rigid interpretation of reported times, a smoothed, running-average curve is superimposed on the histogram. Visual inspection of the latter shows four peaks of relatively high accident occurrence at about 9.30, 11.00, 14.00 and 15.30. Tests of significance of differences within this distribution would have little meaning without much more detailed and complex analysis. One of the preliminaries to such an analysis would be to relate the peak time to the beginning of each work period, i.e. from start of work or from end of meals or tea-breaks. However, since some of the tea-breaks were 'unofficial' as well as optional, their timing cannot be given accurately nor do they necessarily apply to all operatives. The working day is then divided into four work spells (indicated by arrows). When the corresponding accident frequencies from each of the day's work periods are grouped by time elapsed since the start of the period, temporal relations of accident occurrence may be seen. The smoothed data of Figure 17 can be arranged according to whether or not these 'unofficial' tea-breaks had been taken. This is shown in Figures 18 and 19.

509 In both cases when the four (or five) frequencies pooled into each 15 min.

Figure 17 Distribution throughout the day of reported times of accident occurrence, grouped in 15 min. intervals (smoothed, running average curve superimposed)

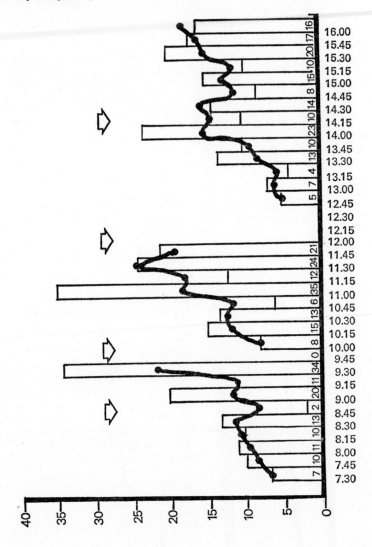

interval are averaged, the number of accidents reported rises steadily throughout the work period. It is assumed, then, that the observed peaks are not altogether artefacts of reporting but represent a genuine phenomenon.

510 The most obvious explanations for the peaks would be that they are either merely the results of continued exposure to risk or that they are in some way a reflection of fatigue or some similar factor resulting in deterioration of operative performance. Neither explanation is very useful at this stage. What constitutes a risk and the concept of risk-taking in this practical every-day situation is still quite unexplored and the nature of 'mental fatigue' as applying to light, repetitive industrial work is not well enough understood. In view of the cautions expressed in the classical studies by Wyatt and his colleagues of the IHRB, as well as since then by many others, e.g. Murrell (1965), Welford (1968), it is perhaps wiser to concentrate on closer study of the phenomena.

VARIABILITY OF PERFORMANCE – SPEED

511 To extend further the area of the foreseeable in the factory work situation in regard to accidents, it can be taken as axiomatic that operative performance is always variable. Field studies to measure variability are few and reports conflicting, but many laboratory studies have shown that performance, even of well-motivated subjects, varies measurably in speed and accuracy, in the course of one to three-hours work spells, tending to show decline in either or both. Much of this variability is quite outside deliberate control of the subject and perhaps even outside his awareness.

512 The following observations were taken to obtain additional information on the variability of speed. Accuracy will be considered later.

Method of observation
513 The observer had been attached for some months to the accident research team in the factory, had conducted an ergonomic analysis of most work stations on the lines described by Corlett, Davies, Knight, Rowe & Smith (1967) and had discussed with most of the operatives and staff various environmental factors of noise, temperature and lighting. All concerned were therefore well acquainted with the observer's presence and with the fact that he frequently carried scientific equipment around the workshop. For the present purpose, he carried a small portable tape-recorder (Ficord) with a suction cup (telephone type) attachment. With the agreement of all concerned he took 'recordings of machine noise', fixing the attachment as close as possible to the cutting or component-holding part of the machines with minimal interference in operations. Records were taken from small and large capstan lathes and the operatives' tasks were all self-paced.

514 The minimum duration of recording was 50 uninterrupted work cycles, taking up to 12 minutes. During this time the observer monitored the sound with a stethoscope earphone. He stood as far as possible out of the operative's line of sight or with his back turned, to avoid the impression that he was watching his performance. The times of day during which recordings were obtained derived

Figure 18   Smoothed data from Figure 17: frequencies re-grouped by beginning of work period (assumed that tea-break taken at 08.45 hours)

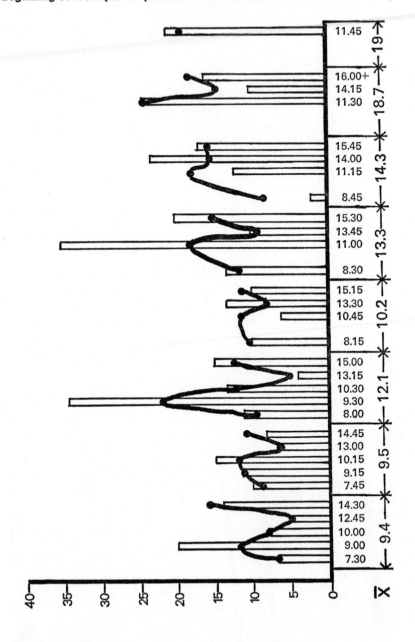

Figure 19   Same as Figure 18: assumed that no tea-break taken at 08.45 hours and worked through to 09.45 hours

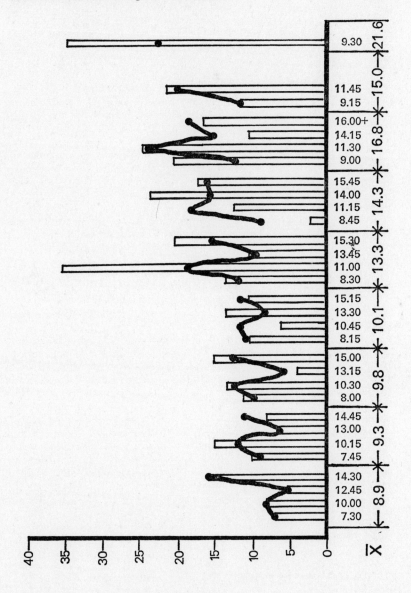

from the data in Figure 17: viz:

Fore Period	Critical Period
08.30 – 09.15	09.15 – 09.45
10.30 – 11.00	11.00 – 11.30
13.15 – 13.45	13.45 – 14.20
14.45 – 15.15	15.15 – 15.50

Recording was carried out over 16 weeks on Tuesdays, Wednesdays and Thursdays, days of the week when accident frequency, corrected for absences, was found to be slightly more critical that at the beginning or end of the week (J. Martin, pers. comm.).

515 The subjects of observation were capstan lathe operators, one man and three women, all with over 10 years' service and therefore thoroughly practised in the work.

Method of analysis
516 Immediately after recording, a description of the work cycle was noted so that the various clicks recorded on the tape could be identified in terms of parts of the cycle, for example 'load', 'engage clutch', 'cut', 'reverse' etc.

517 The tapes were later played back and the time intervals between clicks measured with a stop watch. The data resulting from this were the times taken for each part of the work cycle. Their variability was estimated by a form of auto correlation, Mean Square Successive Difference (Von Neumann, Kent, Bellinson & Hart, 1941) and a measure derived from this, the Coefficient of Variation over Time (CVT) (see Burdick & Scarbrough, 1968). This measure expresses the difference between one movement and the preceding one as a percentage ratio. It is thought to have greater stability than auto correlation and appears to be more appropriate to time series than the ordinary Coefficient of Variation when base line data are not available.

Output
518 Mean cycle times, and total times taken to complete 50 work cycles, were compared as between the four work-periods of the day. No significant differences were found. This comparison was made as a check on consistency of performance and not as an estimate of output rate, since cycle times as measured here cannot be regarded as a valid sample for work study measures.

Variability
519 The overall variability scores of cycle times was found to rise slightly over the day from 0·269 in the first period to 0·317 in the last, an increase of 18·2 per cent.

520 The CVT's for the loading and cutting parts of cycles were computed separately for each occasion and averaged over the four operatives for each period. Figure 20 compares mean variability over 600 cycle times (4 operatives ×

3 days × 50 cycles each) during fore and critical periods respectively. It will be seen that loading times are about twice as variable as cutting times throughout the day. In the early afternoon, cutting times seem to have become less variable, whereas loading variability remained high, especially during the critical periods. It would require a larger sample of observations on other subjects before more general conclusions could be drawn about speed of performance of other than those observed. Nevertheless, this method of analysis helped to pinpoint one of the major sources of variability for further investigation.

Figure 20   Mean variability of cycle time during fore and critical periods of accidents occurrence

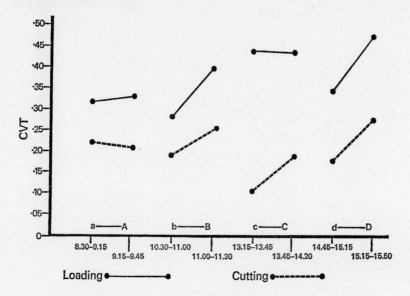

VARIABILITY OF ACCURACY IN PERFORMANCE
A CASE STUDY

521   The second relevant finding of the NIIP accident research team had been that the risk of injury to the operatives' hands was much greater than that to any other part of the body. Of the 427 accidents under review here, 385 (90·2 per cent) were to the hands, almost equally divided between right and left. This quantitative evidence confirms what is, of course, intuitively known to be the case in this kind of industrial work, despite frequent supervision and the fitting of guards and other mechanical safety arrangements. The quality of these in this factory was, perhaps, somewhat above the general average. There will always be an element of risk to the hands in lathe work, grinding, stamping and drilling, unless fully automated machinery is devised. Meanwhile, closer study of hand movements is indicated.

522   In the present context, the intention was twofold: to identify in detail the reasons for the variability observed in the previous section, and to provide data permitting treatment in terms of measures currently used in the experimental investigation of human skills.

523   One such task description in the form of a sensorimotor process chart is presented as an illustrative case study. (For a recent review of method, see Cunningham & Duncan, 1967 and Annett & Duncan, 1967.)

Task description
524   This operation on a Mikron capstan lathe, carried out by one of the women from the group observed in the previous section, was self-paced and consisted of applying a cutting tool to a cylindrical component, $1\frac{1}{2}$ in. long, with a diameter of 0·236 in. The work study description was:

> '*Re-centre squared end, face to length and chamfer o/dia.* Pick up pieces and load to collet, clamp by handle left hand. Machine running. Advance turret right hand, centre face and chamfer o/d, relieve turret. Release collet and remove finished part to box.'

The observer's description of the same task is set out, for each hand separately, in Table 30. Eleven movement elements are distinguishable, numbered in their timing sequence. As far as possible, this sequence is preserved in the lay-out of the table and if both hands move simultaneously this is shown in the same row. It will be noted that the division into 'load' and 'cut' made previously is represented here by movements numbered 2 to 6 and 7 to 10 respectively.

525   A break-down of the operative's average output, observed over three days, is as follows:

Output	Hand Movements
770 pieces per hour	8,470 movements per hour
12·8 pieces per min.	140·8 movements per min.
or 1 piece in 4·68 secs.	1 movement in 0·43 secs.

Information processing
526   Research on skilled performance of the kind considered here has recently been reviewed by Welford (1968), who suggests that complex patterns of movement normally involved in everyday activities follow the same principles as the basic ones studied in the laboratory. The problem is now to apply these measures to performance in the field such as the present case. Since the work situation is one in which the sedentary operative does not engage in intense bodily activity, it is appropriate to treat the operation in terms of *information processing* rather that as transformation of physical energy. If this operation is regarded as a compound of targeting tasks, i.e., a special case of reciprocal tapping combined with repeated smaller moves of high accuracy, then the 'rate of gain of information' might be measured. An operational index, combining speed and accuracy into a single score, is available in Fitt's formula, as modified by Welford (1968):

$$\text{Movement time} = \text{Log}^2 \frac{A}{W} + \cdot 5$$

where A is the amplitude of movement and W the width of target within which the movement is required to end. A correction for errors can be applied (Crossman, 1957). However, as will be seen later, the percentage of errors was too small to be significant for the present purpose. It is considered that the frequencies of movements and their time-scale bear sufficiently close resemblance to those in laboratory studies to justify applying this measure. An additional assumption to be made is that movement times in such a compound task, expressed in bits, are simply additive. Although this is not known to have been tested, it is made here as a convenient working assumption.

527 Having identified the elements, the classifications in Table 30 attempt to answer, by observation, the following questions:

(a) What determines the start of the movement? This concerns the signals or cues required for the movement to commence and the expected sense modality.

(b) What determines the distance of travel of the hand, and width of target area? In the case of surface targets the latter is relatively easy to measure. If the target was, however, a lever, the procedure was to measure the effective width of the part of the hand which hit the lever.

(c) What decides the ending of the movement?

528 To answer this third question distinction has to be made between ballistic and controlled movements. In the former, the hand is 'thrown' rapidly with apparently constant force against a target (lever or surface) and the movement stops on impact with the target area, no specific decision to stop or slow down being needed. In the latter, an object (component or lever) is moved deliberately with graduated force, requiring decisions about speed and the ending of the movement. In ballistic movements, due to the speed of the hand, no corrections of the trajectory appear to be possible once the movement has started. The movement is, therefore, 'open-loop' and its accuracy depends upon previously built-up skill. It is now suggested that, since such movements are somewhat removed from direct cognitive control, they may provide an index of the operating condition of the person performing in the situation under review. In skills which have been so well trained that they have become automatic, this index may be specifically sensitive to variations in underlying control functions.

OBSERVATION OF HAND MOVEMENTS

529 While compiling Table 30, certain incidents likely to contribute to variations in performance were observed and noted in the remarks column. These became the basis for the following series of observations. Each such incident was regarded

Table 30 – Process Chart
Left Hand

Element of Operation	Distance of Travel and Width of Target	Response Cue Sense Modality	Decision	Remarks
1. From front work surface picks new component with thumb/index finger	Negligible	Touch/Visual identifies 'flat' end of component or alternatively knurled end	Search Grasp Flat/Knurled	'Groping' movement sometimes slow
2. Opens collet clamp by pushing lever away with back or underside of hand while still holding new piece with thumb/index finger	3 cm to pneumatic clamp lever W=10 cm	Touch Mechanical stop on lever	Ballistic move Stop?	Lever some times misse Componen hot, some- times fails extract at first attem
4. Brings hand near to collet and passes new piece to R.H.	40 cm to near collet W=2 cm	Touch/Visual +Kinesthetic R.H. has grasped	Controlled move Stop Release hold	Sometimes fails to gra immediatel Sometimes 2–3 or mo attempts at insertion
6. Brings hand back to clamp lever, pulls it towards self, closing collet	40 cm to clamp lever W=5 cm	Touch comp. driven home Kinesthetic mechanical stop on clamp lever	Ballistic move (Stop?) Pull Stop?	Sometimes fails to touc lever at first attempt
9. Picks up next piece as in element 1 above	36 cm. to front work surface W=10 cm		Ballistic move (Stop?)	

Right Hand

Decision	Response Cue Sense Modality	Distance of Travel and Width of Target	Element of Operation
	Visual/Kinesthetic	43 cm to near collet W=12 cm	Applies tool in previous cycles. Hand releases turret lever
Collet shut or open?	Complex Component stops turning as clamp opens, but lathe keeps turning	15 cm	3. Removes previous comp., grasps, pulls and throws in box
Grasp This end in first or turn piece around? Insert comp. Stop	Touch/Visual knurled or flat end of comp. felt or seen Complex Touch Comp. entering hole begins to turn with collet. Mechanical stop in collet	5 cm	5. Rests underside of hand on toolstock for position, grasps new component with thumb/index at nearest end. Then, according to orientation of comp., either turns it or not; then aims into collet and pushes comp. into hole with top of thumb
Ballistic move (Stop?)	Kinesthetic Turret to lever extended to mechanical stop	43 cm to turret lever W=12 cm	7. Hand to turret lever; twisting wrist and stretching fingers from beneath lever
Controlled move Stop	Complex Kinesthetic, mechanical stop, on turret	10 cm tool travel W=10 cm	8. Advances turret, pulling lever towards self from below
Release lever Ballistic move (Stop?)	Mechanical return by spring (rubber band)	43 cm to near collet W=12 cm	10. Release lever which springs back 11. Hand returns to near collet and element 3 above

as a deviation from the standard pattern set out in the Table and classed as an 'Unsuccessful Hand Movement' (UHM). For instance, if the hand at the end of a ballistic movement fails to grasp the lever, or if the insertion of the component into the collet requires more than one attempt, the initial movement can be said to have been insufficiently accurate or unsuccessful.

530   Such deviations from normal performance could occur at random intervals and be truly unpredictable. On the other hand, the operative's movement control functions may deteriorate (quite without her awareness) with time since last break, and it was therefore of interest to establish the distribution of UHM's over the work period.

Method of observation
531   The operative observed was one of the four whose performance was reported on in the previous section, and the task is described in Table 30. The reason for choosing this particular operative was that she was among the three in this workshop who had the highest number of reported accidents ($N = 17$) in the preceding two years.

532   For various reasons, observations for periods longer than an hour at a time were not feasible and so the times chosen were the critical hours of the day (see above). Again, the operative was observed in each period on three occasions. Having obtained her consent to being watched for an hour at a time, the observer seated himself about three yards from the work station, out of the operative's immediate line of vision but so that both hands could be seen. He sat as still as possible, avoiding sudden movements, and counted the numbers of UHM's, noting them on a form at the end of each five-minute period. This procedure was intended to reduce the likelihood that the operative would detect which events were noted down.

RESULTS AND DISCUSSION

Unsuccessful hand movements ('Errors')
533   The mean number of UHM's observed during the critical hours of three consecutive days were as follows:

Period	per hour	Unsuccessful Hand Movements per 5 min. spell	
		Mean	SD
(a) 08.45 – 09.45	127·1	10·60	5·00
(b) 10.45 – 11.45	149·4	12·45	4·64
(c) 13.15 – 14.15	131·4	10·95	3·66
(d) 14.45 – 15.45	120·1	10·00	3·03

534   Broadly speaking, therefore, the frequency of UHM's was –
      130 per hour
      2·1 per min.
or one in 28 secs. or one for every six components produced.

535 The distribution over the 12 five-minute spells of the critical hours is shown in Figures 21 (a) to (d), each point representing the mean of three observations of one operative. Figure 22 shows the results of averaging the four work periods of the day. The grand mean level over the day (10·9 UHMs per 5 min.) is indicated in these graphs by a broken line. In the second work period (10.45–11.45)

Figure 21 (a) to (d) Distribution of Unsuccessful Hand Movements over five-minute spells during each of the four critical hours.

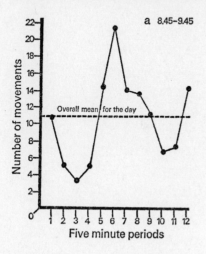

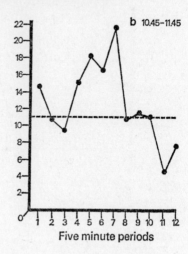

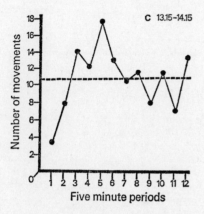

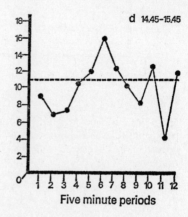

the increase over the day's mean was 15 per cent. To test on this relatively small sample whether the distribution within the hour could have been random, the hours were sub-divided into quarters and it was hypothesised that more UHMs would occur in the second and third quarter than in the first and last. This rank-ordering is confirmed at the 0·001 level of confidence (L=118, Page, 1963).

Figure 22   Data from Figure 21: the four work-periods of the day averaged

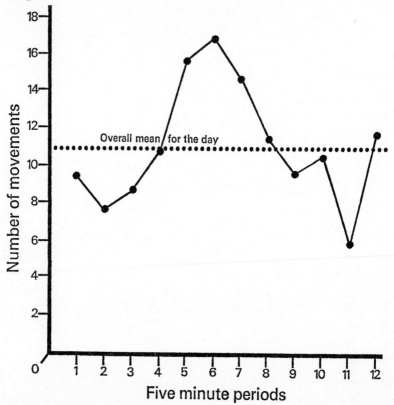

536 The frequency of UHMs can now be put into the perspective of the whole performance over an hour. Out of a total of 8,470 hand movements made by this operative in an hour, 98·46 per cent were carried out correctly and UHMs represented only 1·54 per cent. (In another series of similar observations of a different operation by another operative the 'error rate' was found to be 1·60 per cent.) That is to say that, at the peak time of UHM occurrence, a 15 per cent increase represents only 1·77 per cent of all movements made.

537 The complex loading movement No. 5, part of which is basically a simple aiming task, namely to insert the component into the collet, appeared to be most frequently unsuccessful. This difficulty will be appreciated when the dimensions are considered. The inner diameter of the target area in the collet in its open position was 0·250 in. (6·350 mm) and the component's outer diameter was 0·236 in. (6·00 mm), the difference being 0·014 in. (0·350 mm) or a tolerance of only 5·5 per cent.

Rate of information gain

538 Applying the modified formula to each of the seven ballistic movements in the operation and summing the results yields approximately 18·7 bits. Equally, the pin-insertion movement No. 5, appears to be identical with an experiment in which Schouten *et al.* (see Welford, 1968, p. 153) estimated the information transmitted at about 12 bits. The total score for the observed task would, there-fore, be about 30·7 bits in 4·67 secs., and the rate of gain 6·6 bits per sec.

539 In this estimate, unsuccessful movements, or 'errors' of the order of 1·54 per cent might seem to be immaterial. However, the assumption that these hand movements were all ballistic is very conservative; closed-loop controlled movements are likely to require more information processing, including that of proprioceptive feedback. Singleton (1953) found that it was not the speed of actual movement but the time between one movement and the next which increased with time on task and it was thus the deciding which way to move that slowed performance. UHM's can, therefore, be seen as a breakdown of semi-automatic activity, interrupting the flow of signals and responses so that separate decisions are needed where previously larger units of behaviour were adequately controllable.

Unsuccessful hand movements and accidents

540 As was to be expected from the results of laboratory studies, repetitive performance in the workshop was found not to be completely stereotyped even after years of practice. Moreover, a tendency for increases in variability of speed, i.e. irregularity of performance, was observed during those periods which were critical for accident occurrence. The case study showed further that during the same periods UHM's also tended to increase. It is clear that UHM's contribute to irregularity in speed, particularly if they mean repeating part of a movement. The time round about 11.00 hrs is of particular concern and it is likely that at this time the 15 per cent increase in UHM's relates to the 35 per cent increase in both loading and cutting times. On the other hand, some of the UHM's may be less 'dangerous' than others; e.g. missing the tool transport handle (Element No. 7 in Table 30) is less likely to bring injury than fumbling while loading the component into the collet. especially if the latter rotates. Nevertheless, since the ballistic move to the tool lever depends so much upon previously accumulated skill, increasingly frequent misses here may well be the advance warning of an impending wider deterioration of performance.

541 The question must now be put whether the accident frequency peaks were merely a function of prolonged exposure to risk or whether they were more likely to be connected with 'fatigue'. The data collected by observation render the assumption of a genuine deterioration more plausible than the mere duration of time at work, because both variability of speed and UHMs are at least somewhat reduced towards the end of the critical hourly period.

542   However, for a number of reasons it is unlikely that this deterioration is fatigue in the sense usually understood. As said above, the operative is unlikely to expend a great amount of physical energy, certainly not to the point of exhaustion, after even $8\frac{1}{2}$ hours at this kind of self-paced work. Any decrement in performance is thus more likely a matter of 'mental load' than specifically one of changes in psychomotor control functions. Even so, provided other work aspects are normal and the operative is not under stress, the work load is not great. For over 98 per cent of the time, when movements are well co-ordinated, information transmission at 6·6 bits per sec. did not seem to be overly stressful. Whatever deterioration in performance does occur is not likely to be due to continuous overloading of the operative's capacity. Rather the situation would generally seem to be one of monotony or underloading. In such a situation, the relatively unvarying nature of the repetitive task would lead to temporary shifts in sensitivity and loss of information from feedback. As the timing of movements becomes then disorganised, the rhythm is broken and single movements have to be made under separately controlled conditions. In such a case, information cannot be processed at a rate of more than about two bits per sec. and the operative would tend to become overloaded.

543   It may also be that just during the transition from ballistic to deliberate movements, for a fraction of a second, no strict control over the hand is exercised and that this could be the moment when accidental injury ensued.

544   The diagnosis of monotony being operative in this task is lent still greater force when the general bodily state of the operatives at the peak accident times of the day is taken into account. The peaks of frequency of UHMs occurred at about 09.15, 11.20, 13.40 and 15.15 hrs. This is respectively 105, 80, 55 and 60 minutes after the start of work periods. The highest peaks of both accidents and UHM's occur at about 11.00–11.30 hrs. Recent findings on performance curves in relation to circadian rhythms of body temperature are likely to be relevant.

545   'It has been found in shiftwork experiments that it is over this period (between 07.00–08.00 and 10.00–11.00) during which temperature rises by 0·56°F, that the most marked and consistent improvements in performance efficiency are observed.' (Colquhoun, Blake & Edwards, 1968.) From about 11.00 onwards then, when efficiency, as measured by calculation tests and vigilance performance, rises normally to a high level (until about 20.00 hrs), the periods of relatively error-free performance on the shop floor tended to become shorter. UHM's – and accident peaks – occurred then, at least in this study, at a time when the body is, so to speak, more efficient than the task demands. 'Mental fatigue' would result from over-loading, with many unexpected signals arriving in quick succession. By contrast, in the present task almost no signals are unpredictable, either in timing or in novelty. Variations in machine performance (stiffness, warm-up effects, speed, wear of tools) would appear to have been small, and so were variations in consistency of materials used (brittleness, hardness). It should be added that this particular task was by no means the most monotonous job in that workshop.

546 In conclusion, it should be emphasised that only a small facet of light engineering factory work was studied here and any generalisation from the results of these observations would be premature. Even so, the tasks observed were not untypical. As to implications for accident research, the search for performance variables which can be studied 'irrespective of their consequences' may yield further evidence to narrow down the area of the genuinely unpredictable, or random, elements in accident causation. In regard to accident prevention, the practical problems arising seem to be at least as much organisational as technical. It seems doubtful whether briefer periods of work, interspersed with more rest pauses, could alleviate the boring nature of the jobs. If anything, a greater variety of rather dissimilar operations may reduce the longer-term monotony. Perhaps more rewarding, but much more difficult to achieve, might be the attempts at finely graduated increases in complexity of operations with more deliberate additions to the operative's exercise of skill and discretion in method of operations and in task assignment.

ACKNOWLEDGEMENT

547 The author wishes to acknowledge with thanks the help provided by the members of the accident investigating team of the National Institute of Industrial Psychology, London, England.

REFERENCES

ANNETT, J. & DUNCAN, K.D. (1967). Task analysis and training design. *Occup. Psychol.*, **41**, 211–222.

BURDICK, J. A. & SCARBROUGH, J. T. (1968). Heart rate and heart rate variability. *Percept. Mot. Skills*, **26**, 1047–1053.

COLQUHOUN, W. P., BLAKE, M. F. J. & EDWARDS, R. S. (1968). Experimental studies of shiftwork – I. *Ergonomics*, **11**, 437–454.

CORLETT, E. N., DAVIES, B. T., KNIGHT, A. A., ROWE, R. & SMITH, R. (1967). An investigation into the ergonomics of open-fronted presses. *Ergonomics*, **10**, 389–398.

CROSSMAN, E. R. F. W. (1957). The speed and accuracy of simple hand movements, quoted in Welford, A. T. (1968). *Fundamentals of Skill.* London: Methuen.

CUNNINGHAM, D. J. & DUNCAN, K. D. (1967). Describing non-repetitive tasks for training purposes. *Occup. Psychol.*, **41**, 203–210.

MCFARLAND, R. A. (1963). A critique of accident research. *Ann. N. Y. Acad. Sci.*, **107**, 686–695.

MURRELL, K. F. H. (1965). *Ergonomics.* London: Chapman & Hall.

PAGE, E. B. (1963). Ordered hypotheses for multiple treatments: A significance test for linear ranks. *J. Amer. Statist. Ass.*, **58**, 216–230.

SINGLETON, W. T. (1953). Deterioration of performance on a short-term perceptual-motor task. In *Symposium on Fatigue* (ed. W. F. Floyd and A. T. Welford). London: Lewis.

SUCHMAN, E. A. (1961). A conceptual analysis of the accident phenomenon. Quoted in McFarland, R. A. (1963). A critique of accident research. *Ann. N. Y. Acad. Sci.*, **107**, 686–695.

VON NEUMANN, J., KENT, R. H., BELLINSON, H. R. & HART, B. I. (1941). The mean square successive difference. *Ann. Math. Statist.*, **12**, 153–162.

WELFORD, A. T. (1968). *Fundamentals of Skill*. London: Methuen.

Appendix 23
Climatic factors

548 At all the shops we used a thermohygrograph to record dry bulb temperature and humidity continuously, and reference to the charts told us the values of each at the time of an accident.

549 We used dry and wet bulb temperatures in our analysis of temperature effects, because we considered more specialised measures such as effective temperature, which takes air velocity into consideration, to be unnecessary in three shops and impractical in the despatch department.

550 The air velocity in the three shops was low and did not vary appreciably. Localised draughts did occur in some positions, but these were irregular. In the despatch department we measured air velocities ranging from nearly zero to over 100 ft/min. The velocity appeared to be dependent on the direction of the wind outside, as more places on one side of the shop were open to the outside than on the other. The variations in velocity were such that we could not reliably estimate effective temperature at the time and position of an accident, and the wide variety of clothing worn would have added further inaccuracy. For these reasons, we considered a scale of effective temperature to be impractical at this shop.

551 At three of our shops we analysed the relationship of dry bulb temperature and accidents. We are aware that wet bulb temperature is a more reliable measure of the condition of the human body, which reacts rather like a wet bulb. We hope to publish, at a later date, a separate paper which will contain analysis of the relationship between wet bulb temperature and accidents in these three shops.

552 From a sample of the thermohygrograph readings we found the frequency of occurrence of different dry bulb temperatures and levels of humidity. We did this for three of the shops by taking the average temperature level of humidity over a two-hour period for each day of the study. The two-hour periods were taken consecutively so that the analysis covered the whole of the working day. We grouped the frequencies into temperature ranges of 1°C and humidity ranges of 5 per cent. The number of accidents within each range could then be compared with the number of times those ranges appeared in the samples of temperatures and humidities.

553 We calculated the ratio of the accidents occurring in each range of temperature or humidity to the frequencies of occurrence of each range. The histograms (Figures 23–28) illustrate the results obtained. In some cases the extremes of temperature and humidity did not occur in the sample, or there were no accidents in some of the extreme categories, so these have been added to neighbouring categories to allow the ratios to be calculated.

554 We used t-tests to determine whether the mean dry bulb temperature at the times when accidents occurred was significantly different from the mean dry bulb temperature over the whole of the study period, and similarly for humidity.

Table 31 – Temperature and Humidity

Dry Bulb Temperature	Shop A	Shop B	Shop C
t	5·70	7·49	1·70
d.f.	756	933	399
p	1%	1%	n/s
Humidity			
t	4·14	1·67	1·04
d.f.	920	967	407
p	1%	n/s	n/s

555 The cases where we found significant values show fairly consistent downward trends (see Figures 23–28). The results show that at shops A and B more accidents occurred at lower temperatures than would be expected from the distribution of temperatures during the studies. At shop A more accidents occurred at lower humidities than would be expected. At shop B it appears from Figure 26 that more accidents occurred at extremes of humidity, but this trend was not found to be significant. Temperature and humidity did not appear to affect accidents at shop C.

556 For the despatch department the analysis was different because there were fewer accidents and a greater range of temperature and humidity. One of the reasons for the choice of this shop was the large climatic variation we could expect. The walls had nine large openings where roads entered the shop. Thus the climatic conditions in the department were similar to those outside, and during our study we recorded wet bulb temperatures ranging from −5°C to +30°C and humidities ranging from 37 per cent to 100 per cent.

557 In this shop we had discovered a direct relationship between the work load and number of accidents (see Appendix para. 327) and so we isolated the work factors before studying the effect of climatic conditions on accidents. We took the period between 10 am and 12 noon, which included both shifts and a fairly constant work load. The work load at other periods varied rather more, the early morning and late evening usually being very busy but sometimes quite slack, and the afternoon usually being very slack but sometimes quite busy.

Shop A

Figure 23   Accidents and temperature

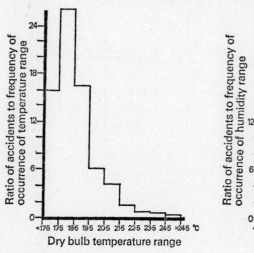

Figure 24   Accidents and humidity

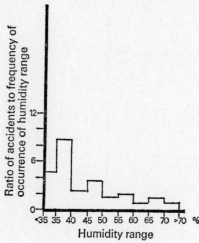

Shop B

Figure 25   Accidents and temperature

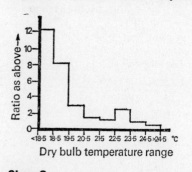

Figure 26   Accidents and humidity

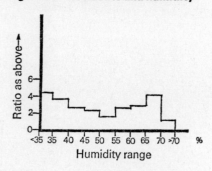

Shop C

Figure 27   Accidents and temperature

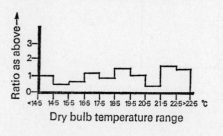

Figure 28   Accidents and humidity

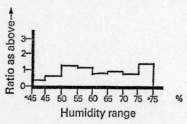

Despatch department
Figure 29   Accidents and dry bulb temperature

Figure 30   Accidents and wet bulb temperature

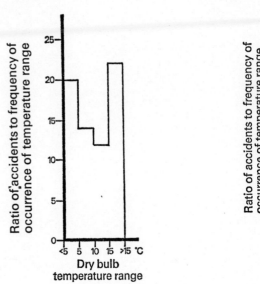

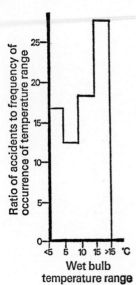

Figure 31   Accidents and humidity

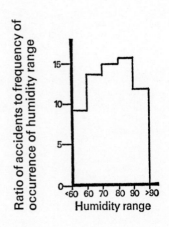

558   We were therefore able to find:

(*a*)   The number of times wet and dry bulb temperature fell into 5°C categories between 10 am and 12 noon.

(*b*)   The number of times humidity fell into 10 per cent categories between 10 am and 12 noon.

(*c*)   The number of men working on those occasions.

(*d*)   The number of accidents sustained by the men on those occasions.

(*e*)   The corrected frequency of accidents, i.e., the number of accidents which would have occurred if an equal number of men had been exposed to each climatic category on an equal number of occasions (see Figures 29–31).

559   Using a t-test, we tested the difference between the number of accidents that occurred within each climatic category and the corrected frequency of accidents. The results, shown in Table 32, were not statistically significant, but this may be because the small numbers precluded adequate analysis.

Table 32 – Results of t-test

	Wet Bulb Temperature	Dry Bulb Temperature	Humidity
N	66	66	66
t	6·44	4·06	1·51
d.f.	3	3	4
p	n/s	n/s	n/s

560   As shown in Figure 30, more accidents appeared to occur at the high temperature extreme in the despatch department. The effect was not clear at the low extremes. This was probably because the men wore sensible warm clothes and gloves in cold weather. Although the gloves were not designed for safety, they did offer some protection against minor cuts to the hands and fingers. The fact that sleeves were rolled down protected the arms and wrists. It was therefore to be expected that we should find only a small climatic effect on accidents at the lower end of the temperature range. In hot weather, the men were able to take off their shirts to keep comfortable. Therefore, in the higher temperature range, we would expect an increase of accidents because the men were wearing no 'protective' clothing.

JEAN MARTIN
M. SIMON

Appendix 24
Noise

561 There was a range of noise levels in our shops from the comparatively quiet (70 dB) during which conversation was easy without raising the voice, to the unpleasantly noisy (100 dB) where conversation was almost impossible. High levels of noise were associated with particular work processes such as press work or shearing. Noise was intermittent or constant depending on the process.

562 We are not able to say whether noise affected accidents in the practical situations we studied at our four shops. We could not compare accidents on the same jobs under quiet conditions and under noisy conditions. The high accident rate in the noisy press shop appeared to be primarily due to the greater risks involved in the tasks performed by the press operators compared with the low accident rate in the quieter gear-cutting shop, where fewer risks were identifiable.

563 In order to study the effect of noise in our shops, we would have needed to know the noise level at the time and position of an accident, the noise level at the same time and position of a first control (doing strictly the same job), and a second control (matched for personal characteristics), and ideally also the noise levels at other positions in the shop. It is essential to know whether the noise is constant or intermittent and, if the latter, in what way intermittent.

564 We found this impossible because the majority of accidents were discovered and recorded after the accident had occurred, even if only a short time after. The only way of finding the noise levels at the times we needed to know them would have been to have fixed a continuously-recording noise meter to every machine. The cost of doing this would of course have been prohibitive.

565 We think that to say 'noise has not yet been shown to have an effect on the number of industrial accidents' is dogmatic and immaterial, for these very reasons that it is both difficult and expensive to study any effect reliably. At the present we must refer to the scientifically-controlled laboratory experiments and assume that what is true in those situations is also very likely to be true in an industrial workshop. Broadbent (1964) observes that errors have been shown to increase at extreme noise levels of above 90 dB. He points out that task is an important factor, i.e., for some simple tasks a noise stimulus may aid attention and decrease the rate of errors, while for other more complex tasks a noise stimulus may have the opposite effect.

566 Many tasks in a factory, although often apparently repetitive and simple, are in reality quite complex. It is only the operator's learned skills that may mislead a naive watcher. Generalising from the laboratory studies, distracting or deafening noise may contribute to accidents if an operator has, for example, to handle sharp-edged components in several ways. Small errors of the handling movements may easily result in a cut to a finger or hand.

RECOMMENDED REFERENCES

BELL, A. (1966) Noise: an occupational hazard and public nuisance. *Public Health Paper* No. 30. Geneva: W.H.O.

BROADBENT, D. E. (1957) Effects of noises of high and low frequency on behaviour. *Ergonomics*, **1**, 21–29.

BROADBENT, D. E. (1964) Noise in industry. *Ergonomics for industry* No. 6. London: D.S.I.R.

BROADBENT, D. E. (1951) Noise, paced performance and vigilance tasks. APU 165/51. Cambridge: Applied Psychology Research Unit.

JARISON, H. J. (1954) Paced performance on a complex counting task under noise and fatigue conditions. *American Psychologist*, **9**, 399–400. (Abstract)

MINISTRY OF LABOUR, (1963). Noise and the worker. *Safety Health and Welfare series* No. 25. London: H.M.S.O.

RICHARDS, E. J. (1965). Noise considerations in the design of machines and factories. (The Fifty-second Thomas Hawksley Lecture) London: Institution of Mechanical Engineers. Also in *Proceedings of the I.Mech.E.* 1965–1966, **180**(1), 1099–1128.

SYMONS, N. S. and others: (1953). Industrial noise. *Factory*, December.

WESTON, H. C. & ADAMS, S. (1935). Performance of weavers under varying conditions of noise. *Industrial Health Research Board Report* No. 70. London: H.M.S.O.

M. SIMON

Appendix 25
Personal factors

567 We collected personal information about the people in our samples at the four shops. The information was gained from personnel records (e.g. application forms) and from our own conversations with people throughout the periods that we were based in their shops.

568 We examined personal information for each person to find whether any relationships existed between personal factors and accident rates. Some of the information about factors was qualitative and subjective and could not be analysed reliably. Other personal factors yielded insufficient data for analysis e.g. too few people were left-handed to give us a reliable sub-group.

569 Table 33 shows the results we obtained and is followed by a brief discussion of the factors studied.

Age
570 At each of the four shops, we analysed the influence of age on accidents by dividing people into high and low accident groups. We then matched each person in the high group with a person in the low group for length of service and used Wilcoxon's Matched Pairs Signed Ranks Test (2-tailed tests) to determine the significance of the age differences between the pairs.

571 In the machine shop, we found that the people in the high accident group were younger than those in the low accident group ($p < 0.05$). However, in the assembly shop, we found the reverse to be true; people in the high accident group were older ($p < 0.03$). We think these are probably task and experience effects (see Appendix paras. 380 and 339) but we do not have sufficient data to prove it.

572 In the mill and the despatch department, we found no differences between the ages of high and low accident people.

573 We also compared the ages of the accident victims with the ages of the first controls, but found no differences between them. However, experience could not be controlled for in this analysis, and as age and experience are highly correlated, we do not think that the analysis is meaningful.

Table 33 – Significance of relationships between accidents and personal factors

Personal factors		Machine	Shop Assembly	Despatch	Mill
Sex	Men	Women	Women	Men	Men
Age	5%(Y)	5%(Y)	3%(Y)	n/s	n/s
Nationality	n/s	n/s	n/s	n/s	—
Marital status	—	n/s	n/s	n/s	—
Dependent children	—	—	—	—	—
Home accidents	0·1%	5%	0·1%	—	n/s
Length of journey to work	n/s	n/s	n/s	n/s	—
Method of journey to work	n/s	n/s	n/s	n/s	—
Height	n/s	n/s	n/s	5%	n/s
Weight	n/s	n/s	n/s	n/s	—
Eyesight	—	—	—	—	—
Handedness	—	—	—	—	—
Smoking	—	—	—	n/s	—
Talkativeness	—	—	—	—	—
Extraversion	5%	5%	n/s	n/s	5%
Neuroticism	n/s	n/s	n/s	n/s	n/s
Intelligence	n/s	n/s	n/s	—	—
Interests	5%	n/s	n/s	—	—
Previous jobs	n/s	n/s	n/s	—	—
Reason for leaving	n/s	n/s	n/s	—	—
Leaving card assessment	n/s	n/s	n/s	X	X
Probationary report	n/s	n/s	n/s	X	X
Manual staff status	—	—	—	X	X
Education	Q	Q	Q	Q	Q
Living accommodation	Q	Q	Q	Q	Q
Medical history	Q	Q	Q	Q	Q
Domestic stress	Q	Q	Q	Q	Q

Key to table:
%: significance level of statistical relationship: the direction of the relationships is discussed in the paragraphs below
n/s: no significant statistical relationship
—: insufficient data and no statistical analysis possible
Q: qualitative data and no statistical analysis possible
X: personal factor not applicable to shop
Y: younger
O: older

Nationality

574 The assembly, machine and despatch shops had high proportions of Irish workers and so we classified people as British, Irish or Other. We controlled

factors of age and experience but found no tendency for nationality to affect accidents in any of the three shops. This is as expected, because nationality may only contribute to accidents if extreme cultural or linguistic differences exist. We noticed few such problems of communication in our shops.

Marital status

575   For the women in the assembly and machine shops, and the men in the despatch department, we chose pairs of people, one married and one single in each pair. They were matched for age and length of service. We compared their accident rates but found no relationship between marital status and accidents. The only relevance of this finding is that it casts doubt on popular theories that arguments with one's spouse cause accidents. Most men in the machine shop and the mill were married, so it was impossible to carry out any comparative analysis there.

Dependent children

576   We thought that having dependent children might be relevant for the women in our study, but so few had any that no statistical analysis was possible.

Home accidents

577   In the machine and assembly shops, we divided people into four groups according to whether they had had none or some accidents at home and at work. In the mill, we divided them as none at home; some at home; less than two at work; two or more at work. (Too few people had no work accidents at all.) In all cases, tests were made on the four groups. These were significant for machine shop men and women, and assembly shop women i.e. those with work accidents were those who had home accidents, but the results for the mill were not significant. So few home accidents were recorded at the despatch department that analysis was not possible.

578   We do not think that this result is evidence of accident proneness. We found that people who talked to us most reported more accidents to us, and were more likely to tell us of their accidents outside work. Therefore, this relationship was to be expected.

Length of journey to work

579   Length of journey to work has commonly been found to be related to labour turnover, those people having long journeys staying only a short time in a firm. In the assembly, machine and despatch shops, we compared length of journeys of pairs of people with high and low accidents matched for length of service. We found no relation between length of journey and accidents. We were not able to obtain data on this factor at the mill.

Method of journey to work

580   We had information on the method of coming to work for the assembly, machine and despatch shops. We found no relation with numbers of accidents (χ^2 test).

Height and weight

581 At the despatch department, we recorded the height and weight of the people in our sample. Controlling for occupational category (because the accident rates of sorters were significantly higher than those of barrowmen and van-packers), we found that people below 5 ft 9 in. height had significantly higher accident rates than those above 5 ft 9 in. ($\chi^2 = 2.59$, df $= 1$ significant at 0.05 level). We think this may be because smaller men had greater difficulty handling goods which were often of awkward dimensions. We found no relationship between accident rate and weight.

582 At the machine and assembly shops, we recorded people's height, and their weights in terms of above average, average and below average for the height and build. We compared the accidents of people who were above and below average in height and in weight but found no relation between those and accidents, using a Mann Whitney U-test.

583 At the mill, we compared the heights of a group of people with less than two accidents with a group with more than two accidents, using a Mann Whitney U-test. We found no significant difference in height between these two groups. However, we did notice a slight trend for the shorter people to have less accidents. This may be related to the fact that equipment and materials were reached by shorter people with greater comfort. Weight data were not available at the mill.

Eyesight

584 We thought that people with uncorrected defects of vision might have more accidents than those with normal or corrected vision, especially in the assembly and machine shops where much of the work was intricate in detail. However, out of a total population of about 800 people in the assembly and machine shops, we discovered only six who should have been wearing glasses and did not wear them. There may have been others who were not aware that they needed glasses or who wore glasses which were not powerful enough. In view of the small number, no analysis was possible.

585 At the despatch department, a full record was kept of each man's medical examination on employment. Eyesight test results were included. We discovered 13 of our 100 people whose vision was worse than 6/12 in one or both eyes, and who did not wear glasses. There may have been more whose eyesight had deteriorated in the years since their medical examination. The 13 people for whom we had evidence of subnormal vision did not sustain more accidents than the others. At this shop, most of the work did not require attention to fine details and minor defects of vision might not have affected accidents.

586 At the mill, we were not able to obtain much information on eyesight, but again the work was not intricate and eyesight was unlikely to be an important factor. There were so few people with colour vision defects that we could not analyse this factor, but normal colour vision was not essential for the work at any of the shops.

Handedness

587 Many machines are designed for right-handed people insofar as the controls are sited on the right hand side of the operator. We therefore asked people at our shops whether they were right or left-handed, but found the data impossible to analyse because an insufficient number of people doing similar tasks were left-handed.

Smoking

588 We found cigarette smoking and accidents impossible to relate. In three of our shops, the populations were too large for us to discover who smoked and how much they smoked. We did not feel that smoking was of sufficient importance to warrant such questions and time. At the one shop where we did discover the number of cigarettes each smoker claimed to smoke daily, we found no tendency for those who smoked, and also no tendency for those who said they smoked over 20 a day, to have a higher accident rate.

Talkativeness

589 Our observers made lists of the people in the assembly shop who talked to them most. Twenty-two people in the assembly shop had no accidents during the whole of our study. Of these, only two were listed as people who talked a lot. Twenty-six people had more than six accidents during the study. Twenty of these were listed as people who talked a lot.

590 In the mill, our observer selected two groups of 25 people, matching them for job titles (NOT task); one group consisted of people who talked to her frequently and the other was a group who were generally less talkative. The accident scores of the two groups over the year of observation were: chatty, 136; not chatty, 44.

591 In the despatch department, chattiness had no effect, as described in Appendix para. 603.

Extraversion and neuroticism

592 We used the Eysenck Personality Inventory (EPI) to investigate the relationship between extraversion and neuroticism and accidents at the four shops.

593 Two samples were selected from accident data derived from the machine shop and the assembly shop. For each of these shops, we chose a high accident group and a low accident group from the people who had been in the shops for the whole study period, plus two months prior to the start of the study. Supervisors were excluded because they were in a different category from the operatives.

594 The original method devised for selecting those two groups was as follows:

(*a*) each shop was treated separately;

(*b*) the names of long term people were extracted;

(c)   these names were arranged in order of number of accidents;

(d)   the top 30 and bottom 30 of the range were picked;

(e)   an attempt was made to select two groups paired for (i) task, (ii) sex, (iii) age and (iv) experience.

595   We hoped to obtain a sample of 50 persons from each shop forming two matched groups of 25, but it was not possible to match for age and task. Pairing was further upset by a number of invited operators not turning up and by one or two who had not been asked but wanted to take part in the tests. Thirty-four people were tested from the machine shop and 28 from the assembly shop.

596   A number of tests were spoiled and regarded as being invalid, and attempts to match pairs in high and low accident groups proved unsatisfactory. The initial statistical analysis was therefore carried out on the following sized samples:

					High	Low	Total
Machine shop	...	...	...	...	18	13	31
Assembly shop	...	...	...	...	17	11	28

597   We used the Mann Whitney U-test to find if the high and low accident groups, taken as representing two independent groups, could have come from the same population. We looked at the EPI extraversion scores and the EPI neuroticism scores, comparing the high and the low accident groups in each shop separately.

598   We did not find a relationship between neuroticism and accidents in either shop, nor between extraversion and accidents in the assembly shop. However, we did find that people in the machine shop with a high number of accidents were significantly more extraverted than those with a low number of accidents $(p < 0.05)$.

599   The Means and the Standard Deviations for the extraversion and neuroticism scores on the EPI were tabulated in order to compare our sample results with those given by Eysenck for (i) a working class group and (ii) a skilled working class group. Work in the machine shop and assembly shop requires varying degrees of skill, and we thought that the scores might be similar to Eysenck's results, possibly falling between his two groups. The comparisons are shown in Table 34 overleaf.

600   Eysenck mentions that correlations with sex are not large, because items giving large sex differences were eliminated in the construction of the inventory. However, there is a tendency for women to score higher than men on N and lower on E, and this may well account for such differences as are shown in the table, between our assembly shop sample (mainly women), and Eysenck's samples.

601   At the mill and despatch shops, we gave the EPI to all who were prepared

Table 34 – Comparison of Eysenck's results with ours on the EPI

Assembly	Sample	Eysenck's Groups 'working class'	'skilled working class'
Extraversion			
Mean	11·0	11·21	12·50
S.D.	4·7	4·40	4·485
Neuroticism			
Mean	11·6	7·765	10·929
S.D.	4·5	4·753	4·446
Machine			
Extraversion			
Mean	12·2	11·2	12·5
S.D.	3·4	4·4	4·485
Neuroticism			
Mean	8·7	7·8	10·446
S.D.	2·8	4·9	4·446

to take it, and were able to analyse the scores in the same way as for the assembly and machine shops. Fifty-one men at the mill took part. We found that people with high extraversion scores (over 12) had sustained significantly more accidents than people with low extraversion scores ($p < 0.05$). We did not find a relationship between neuroticism and accidents.

602   Only 22 men at the despatch department agreed to take the EPI. For the analysis, we excluded 5 men who belonged to the occupational group with a higher accident rate than the other two. We did not find any significant relationships between extraversion or neuroticism, and accidents. (But 17 men is hardly a representative sample.)

603   Too much importance should not be attached to the statistically significant results in the machine shop and the mill. In these two shops, we could not observe all the people easily and so were sometimes unable to notice superficial injuries. To some extent, we relied on people to tell us about their accidents. Less talkative people were more likely not to tell us, and, in some cases, we think we may not have a complete record of all their accidents. The less talkative tended to be more introverted and the more talkative more extraverted, and we think this is the explanation for the results obtained. In the despatch department, where extraversion was not significantly related to accidents, there was a total absence of bias related to talkativeness. The smaller population at this shop was more easily observed and we did not have to rely so much on people telling us about their accidents. Also, since people worked in groups, we sometimes heard about an accident from another member of the group, even if the victim had not mentioned it and we had not noticed it.

Intelligence
604   We gave NIIP Group Test 72 (a test of intelligence in which problems are

presented by means of diagrams built up by domino designs) to the same sample of people at the assembly and machine shops who took the EPI. We found no relationship between their test scores and number of accidents. We did not use this test at the other two shops.

Interests
605 We classified interests as practical, intellectual, physical and other. We managed to collect very little information about people's interests, but did find a relationship between number of accidents and number of other interests among men in the machine shop. We think this is due to the bias of more talkative people telling us about both their accidents and their interests.

Previous jobs
606 We thought that previous experience in other jobs might have some influence on accidents in the assembly and machine shops. In the mill and despatch department, most people had long service; previous jobs, if any, were not relevant. We classified previous jobs of the people in the assembly and machine shop as:

> in same firm,
> same type of work,
> other industrial experience,
> other work experience,
> no previous job.

607 We did not find any relationships between experience obtained in previous jobs and accidents, i.e. a person who had done the same type of work before (even in the same firm) was not less likely to have accidents. This result lends support to the theory that specific task experience is of greater importance in relation to accidents than general experience (see Appendix para. 344–5).

Reason for leaving
608 At two of the shops, we obtained the official reason for leaving given to the personnel department, and in about a third of the cases we asked people who were about to leave why they were leaving. Generally there was agreement between these two. The reasons recorded by the personnel department were classified as:

> transfer,
> domestic,
> pregnancy,
> retired/deceased,
> discharged/dismissed,
> left for better job,
> left of own accord.

This last category was usually dissatisfaction of some kind. By talking to people we were able to break this down further by insufficient money or bonus, friends had moved, bored or wanted a change. These reasons would not be apparent from the personnel records. In the machine shop, we found that reasons indicating dissatisfaction or dismissal were most commonly given by people leaving during their first six months and the other reasons were more common after that. This is found in most companies. Matching for experience, we did not find that people who left had had any more or less accidents than those who stayed.

Leaving card assessment
609 At two of our shops, an assessment of good, average or poor was recorded on a leaving card for people who left. This was used as a guide to whether they would be suitable for re-employment in the future. However, we were only able to obtain this rating in a small number of cases and it did not seem to be related to the number of accidents they had had.

Probationary report
610 In the assembly and machine shops, the relevant supervisors wrote a probationary report on new employees after six weeks. We obtained ratings for people who had joined most recently (about a third of our sample) which covered performance at work and other factors such as timekeeping. The numbers of people getting the different ratings were:

Very good	32
Good	78
Average	48
Fair	11
Poor	1

These ratings did not seem to bear any relation to accidents.

Manual staff status
611 Almost everyone in the assembly and machine shops was given manual staff status after ten years in the company (five years for semi-skilled). There were a few people for whom this was delayed for reasons such as bad time-keeping. We did not analyse this factor as it could not be distinguished from general experience.

Education
612 We tried to collect information about the educational background of people at the four shops. We wanted to know the types of schools attended, length of education and educational interests (e.g. subjects enjoyed at school, post school courses).

613 We were unable to seek any relationships between educational factors and accidents, because we did not have sufficient reliable data. However, we felt that any analysis, even if it were possible, would be irrelevant to accidents. Courses at schools about what to expect in industry are still very few. Most people entering industry for the first time are faced with problems of adjustment, and factors other than educational, such as attitudes, intelligence, type of job and training, will affect the ease with which they can adjust.

614 On a general note, we find it surprising that industry still behaves as if it expects young people to change overnight into steady responsible workers for, say, 40 hours a week (compared with 30 school hours) over 50 weeks a year (compared with 35–40 school-weeks).

Living accommodation

615 A large proportion of the people in three of our shops rented privately-owned accommodation. This is typical of a city population which cannot afford to buy houses or flats, and has not been resident for a sufficient period to qualify for council accommodation.

616 We could not usefully analyse any association between living accommodation and behaviour at work, because we were unable to collect enough information about such things as the space available or the quality of the conditions. Standards of accommodation may influence people in many ways. For example, a man at one of our shops was never late throughout the study period. He regularly arrived at work at least half an hour early in his desire to escape from a tyrannical sister with whom he lived. Another man, involved in a long drawn-out battle with his landlady about maintenance of his flat while she, at the same time, was trying to evict him and his family, suffered a skin disease which his doctor thought was related to his nervous state. He was unfit for some time, part of which he spent in hospital.

Medical history

617 From personnel records, we obtained a picture of people's medical history which, in some cases, was added to during informal conversation. The information was qualitative and we were unable to analyse any relationships with accidents.

618 We also tried to find out whether people had any diseases or disabilities, either temporary or permanent, which might affect their propensity to have accidents. We found that this applied to so few people that we could not come to any reliable conclusions; most people who had accidents had them despite their apparent health!

Domestic stress

619 We obtained information about domestic stress during informal conversation. The information was of a very subjective nature, because a situation which may cause stress to one person may have no effect on another. We did find people with some kind of domestic stress but this did not seem to be related to their accidents in any way.

Conclusion

620 It may be surprising to some that we failed to discover conclusively any personal factors which characterised people who had accidents. We think that the lack of positive results is due to the far greater influence on accidents of exposure to task risk, i.e. the type of work and amount of work done.

JEAN MARTIN
M. SIMON

Appendix 26
Absence and lateness

Machine and assembly shops

621 For the machine and assembly shops data, we used Spearman's rank correlation co-efficient to relate the number of accidents sustained with the number of days of absence both with and without a medical certificate, and number of occasions late. We tested the relationship only for people who had been in the department for the whole of our study so their records were for comparable lengths of time. Almost all the absence with a medical certificate was for sickness, so absence due to accident was not a source of bias. The results are shown below:

Table 35 – Significance of correlation (rho) between accidents and lateness, uncertificated and certificated absence

	Machine shop men	Machine shop women	Assembly women
	(N=67)	(N=44)	(N=99)
Lateness	0·09	0·05	n/s
Uncertificated absence	0·05	0·01	n/s
Certificated sickness absence	n/s	n/s	n/s

622 Frequent lateness and frequent uncertificated absence were associated with frequent accidents in the machine shop, but not in the assembly shop. Certificated absence was not related to accidents in either shop.

623 The lack of any significant results for the assembly women is what we would expect. Both accidents and absence are related to age. The older women had most accidents, but the younger women had more uncertificated absence. However, in the machine shop the younger people had most accidents as well as most uncertificated absence. This probably explains the positive relationship between accidents and uncertificated absence in the machine shop.

Despatch department

624 For this department, we related accident rates to high and low certificated sickness and uncertificated absence, using a Mann Whitney U-Test (Spearman's rho could not be used because of the large number of people with no absence). None of these were significant over the whole sample.

625 The relation between accidents and lateness was not studied as the information on lateness was unreliable. Our observer knew of many instances where people who arrived late were not recorded as being late.

626 There were three main occupational groups at the despatch department, one of which had significantly more accidents that the other two. The comparison of accident rates with absence was therefore repeated for the three groups separately and accident rates for the high accident group were found to be significantly higher for the few people with high uncertificated absence. The explanation for this seems to be that it is the younger, less experienced people who have most uncertificated absence, and, as we have shown (see Appendix para. 339 *et seq.*), less experienced people have more accidents.

627 We also looked at people with extreme accident rates and found that these did have significantly different uncertificated absence rates (χ^2 test $p < 0.05$) but not certificated sickness rates: i.e. the people with very high accident rates had more uncertificated absence than people with very low accident rates or no accidents at all.

Mill

628 At the mill, we were able to obtain figures only for total absence. The figures were not divided according to different types of absence, as at the other shops. As we had no knowledge of the relative proportions of certificated and uncertificated absence, we did not consider it worthwhile to relate total absence to accidents since we would not be able to interpret the results.

JEAN MARTIN

Appendix 27
Sleep and meals

Sleep

629 Over the course of about 1,000 accidents in the assembly shop and the machine shop, we made enquiries about the previous night's sleep of the victims and their controls. We asked for the time spent in bed rather than the amount of sleep which is difficult to estimate.

630 We compared the time spent in bed by the victims with that of their first and second controls, using Wilcoxon's Matched Pairs Signed Ranks Test. Our hypothesis was that the victims would have had less time in bed than the controls, so we were able to use a one-tailed test of significance. The results we obtained are shown below.

Table 36 – Probability values associated with time spent in bed of victims compared with first and second controls

	Assembly women	Machine shop women	Machine shop men
Victims and First Controls	n/s	0·08 (N=31)	0·03 (N=29)
Victims and Second Controls	0·08 (N=118)	0·06 (N=58)	n/s

631 The results show that both men and women victims in the machine shop had less sleep than their first controls, and women in the assembly and machine shop had less sleep than their second controls.

632 At the despatch department and the mill, we did not ask for specific information about the previous night from each accident victim and his controls. Instead, we asked the men in our samples what their usual bedtimes and rising times were for each shift.

633 At the despatch department there was an early shift (08.00–17.00 hrs) and a late shift (11.00–20.00 hrs), and the men alternated between the shifts weekly. Most of the men followed similar routines throughout the study. We found that men spent significantly more time in bed at night in the weeks that they worked on the late shift compared with the time when working on the early shift. Over 80 per cent of the men usually spent more than seven hours in bed at night in their late shift weeks compared with under 30 per cent in their early shift weeks. The tendency was for the bedtime to remain the same, but the rising time to be later when work did not start until 11.00 hrs.

634 Treating each shift separately, we tested the hypothesis that accident rate was related to the usual time spent in bed, but we did not find a statistically significant result.

635 At the mill, there were three shifts. One group of men worked a day shift (08.00–17.00 hrs), and another group alternated weekly between a morning shift (06.00–14.00 hrs) and an afternoon shift (14.00–22.00 hrs). People had least sleep when on the morning shift. There did not appear to be any relationship between sleep and accidents.

Meals
636 We also made enquiries about the meals of the victims and their controls for about 1,000 accidents in the assembly and machine shops.

637 Data on the last meal taken before accidents were obtained from the victims and their controls. The content of the meal was classified as protein, carbohydrate, or both protein and carbohydrate. The size was classified as small, medium or large. We did not find any significant differences between the victims and the controls with respect to either content or size of their last meal before the accident.

638 We thought that, despite not finding a relationship between meals and accidents overall, one might exist between accidents which occurred before the morning break and whether the victim had had breakfast. We therefore compared the victims of accidents before 10.00 with their first controls in respect of whether they had had breakfast and what they had had.

639 We found that almost everyone had had breakfast, despite the early start, and we found no difference between the victims and controls with respect to this, or the size and content of the breakfast.

640 At the despatch department and the mill we asked the men about the meals they usually had.

641 At the despatch department we found that most people had something to eat and drink before they started work on the late shift, but 40 per cent of the people when on the early shift had no food before work and ten per cent had nothing to drink either. A large number of men were therefore in a state of hunger before 9.30 breakfast break, and many comments were made to us to this effect. However, we found no differences between the food prior to work of victims of accidents before the breakfast break and that of others on the same shift.

642   At the mill, there were insufficient people who had little or no food before the start of their shift for any reliable comparisons to be made.

JEAN MARTIN

Appendix 28
Overtime

643 In the machine shop, assembly shop and despatch department, very little overtime was worked and so we could not consider this in relation to accidents.

644 At the mill, the work load fluctuated and weekend overtime was worked when the work load was heavy. We compared the number of accidents per week with the total hours of overtime per week over the whole of our study period. Using Spearman's Rank Correlation Co-efficient, we obtained a value of rho of 0·37 which is significant at the 0·02 level of probability. This shows that accidents were more numerous when more overtime was worked.

645 This result could be explained as a fatigue effect, but we think it is more likely to be connected with the amount of work done. Our observer's impression was that when there was enough work to necessitate overtime, there was a general increase in the pressure of work throughout the week. If people were in fact doing more work, we would expect them to have more accidents (see Appendix 10, para 307 *et seq.*). We could not separate the effect of overtime from the effect of the larger work load which presumably made the overtime necessary.

MARY HALE

Appendix 29
Eye protection for lathe operators

646 In a sample analysis of the records of minor and major accidents, collected in a factory over the course of the past year, we find that foreign body in the eye accounts for something like three per cent of all the injuries. None of the eye injuries resulted from the use of a grinder because this hazard is so well known that appropriate precautions were taken. But many of them occurred to people working various types of lathe.

647 In this country, there is a statutory requirement of eye protection when turning non-ferrous metals or cast iron, if the work is done dry. Details of the statute (The Protection of Eyes Regulations, 1938) can be found in Redgrave's Factories Acts, 21st Edition, page 190 *et seq.* More generally, any employer has a common law duty to take reasonable care for the protection of his workmen, so that if he operates a process where particles are known to be given off and to fly towards the operator, he has an obligation to provide reasonable protection. The interpretation of the word 'reasonable' is, of course, the crux of the matter.

648 Eye risk from a metal cutting process is not usually difficult to recognise. It is often not necessary to look further than the operator's hair, face or upper clothing to see various small metal particles adhering. There are various ways of getting over the problem, the first and the most obvious being to suppress the flying particles at source. The following remarks apply to lathe work but the principles have general application.

Suppression at source
649 If the workpiece is doused under a copious stream of coolant oil, any small splinters of metal given off by the cutting process are carried away in the oil stream. Much grinding is done in this way and so is the turning of steel but materials such as cast iron, brass and some aluminium alloys, often cut better in the dry state. Further, the use of oil or paraffin may carry a risk of dermatitis for the operator so, in general, cutting lubricants are used only where they are really necessary for the cutting, rather than as a means of reducing risk of eye injury.

(Reproduced from NIIP Bulletin, May 1968)

Shielding

650 The best shielding is that which deflects particles in a harmless direction as soon as they have been given off at the cutting point. A small piece of sheet steel, shaped for the purpose, can sometimes be introduced into the tool clamp The further the shield from the tool, the larger the size of shield necessary and it may then become a nuisance because the operator has to move it each time he needs access to the workpiece. It only requires that, on one occasion, the operator does not replace the shield correctly for the eye risk to be re-established. Thus, general shielding between the machine and the operator is not likely to be satisfactory unless it is of the type which is hinged and interlocked with the driving mechanism of the lathe in such a way that its correct position is ensured before the lathe restarts. Such arrangements tend to be expensive but they are found on some automatic machines.

Goggles or safety spectacles

651 All round protection of the eye against flying particles can be obtained by using close fitting goggles but these are usually hot and uncomfortable to wear and are hence relegated to those jobs where the risk is high, for example, welding, grinding and the handling of certain dangerous chemicals. So far as turning is concerned, flying particles come to the operator from the area where the work is being done; the operator is usually looking towards this area, so that spectacles afford quite good protection. The protection can be increased by adding side shields to more or less block the large gap at the side of the lens. Whether or not such spectacles would satisfy the statute, which calls for 'goggles', has not yet been decided, so far as I know, but they are certainly better than nothing. It is difficult, in my experience, to persuade operators to wear anything resembling goggles when working a lathe. There is difficulty, even with spectacles, and this is where we might very well take some lessons from the French.

Fashion may aid function

652 M. Dufay, speaking at the JIMB International Conference held in Paris in May last year (1967), put forward the view that eye protection must either be obviously functional as, for example, in the all enveloping perspex face shield, or fashionably good looking as in the case of spectacles. The part played by fashion is often overlooked in this country where some of the safety spectacles are downright hideous. This is not to say that similar articles cannot be found in France, but certainly a glance at the range of frames available there suggests that the French may be more concerned with appearances than we are. And there is scope for keeping reasonably abreast of fashion, since the life to be expected from a pair of spectacles used under workshop conditions will be only a year or two.

653 Any spectacle wearer will tell you that, to be comfortable, spectacles need to be carefully fitted to the face. Not only is proper fitting necessary for the spectacles to look their best on the face of the worker but it is necessary also to stop them slipping down his nose – a common complaint, particularly amongst those with greasy or perspiring skins. The British Standard on the subject, B.S. 2092, 1962, 'Industrial Eye Protectors for General Purposes', requires that any load-bearing bridge or nose-pad of spectacles shall rest comfortably on the nose and that the side pieces shall be capable of adjustment. It follows that the type of frame must be one which can be bent and generally adjusted to the desired fit. So a factory should carry a limited variety of frames and have someone available who has the modicum of skill required to adjust them if it is going to meet this specification.

654 Once fitted to a particular person, a pair of spectacles will not normally fit anyone else, so each person at risk must keep his own pair by him. The British Standard strongly recommends that cases be supplied along with spectacles. There is sometimes a problem of what to do with them overnight; in one factory I visited things left overnight at the workplace were said to be claimed by the night shift as their own. This might not be the case with spectacles if the night shift were similarly equipped, but there should be provision for keeping spectacles safe overnight, say, in the individual's tool box. It is better to take some care over this than to let people get into the habit of carrying spectacles home, where they would almost certainly be transferred to the wrong jacket pocket or left in the wrong handbag and then not be available when they are needed at work the next day. I have seen a machine shop where everyone wore spectacles all the time but I forgot to ask what happens when somebody mislays his own pair. I generally find mine tucked down beside the cushions on the settee!

655 One factory recently took our advice about fashion and offered a group of lathe operators a choice of spectacles from a variety of modern-looking types. Workers were obliged to choose one frame on which the factory could standardise, which is not quite what we had hoped for; we wanted the choice to be a permanent feature. However, they chose a semi-library frame which suits most of them well and which we notice is now widely worn. The incidence of foreign bodies in the eye seems to have dropped. We hope to be able to review the situation later and determine the long term effects.

Post-script
656 We did visit the workshop again some months later. The pattern of behaviour which seemed to be emerging was that some operators wore the spectacles all the time and other operators wore them only for jobs which they saw as carrying an eye risk. Thus operators' value judgments, which can be erroneous, were having an effect. The supervision did not bother with the spectacles and the wearing of them was not made a condition of employment, neither was it encouraged by the supervision. Thus, in one way, you can regard this experiment as a failure. We thought it a superb illustration of supervisory failure. Very little encouragement was needed to get the operators to put on their spectacles. Several of us did it on several occasions. The supervision seemed quite unaware of what important effects they could achieve by comparatively trivial means.

657 It would have been very instructive if we had had the observers available to carefully watch this section all the time and note which operators removed their glasses for which tasks. But such close-up studies require weeks of careful preparation and are extremely expensive.

P. I. POWELL

Appendix 30
Supervisor favouritism

658 In one of our shops, we found that the supervisors distributed jobs in such a way as to favour some people and not others. The supervisors considered the people they favoured to be harder-working and more reliable than the others, and thought that jobs given to these people were completed more quickly and efficiently.

659 The jobs at this shop were quite varied in nature. On some 'good' jobs, it was possible to earn high bonus in the short time period necessary to complete them, whereas on other more complex jobs, the bonus was low because they took much longer to complete. The majority of jobs fell somewhere between these two extremes.

660 We observed that the supervisors gave the people they favoured a higher proportion of 'good' jobs. They felt that these people were the more useful members of the shop, and should therefore be 'encouraged' to remain by having the opportunity to earn good money.

661 The favoured people sometimes earned up to £10 more a week than the unfavoured ones. Obviously some bad feeling was generated as a result.

662 We found that the measurement of work used for bonus purposes was inversely related to accidents, i.e. the people who were paid most had significantly fewer accidents.

663 We think this is because nearly all the 'good' jobs were safe ones with few inherent risks of injury. Some of the more complex jobs, however, carried patently greater risks. We were able to measure exposure to some of the risks quantitatively, and discovered that the unfavoured people were more exposed to certain risks and had more accidents from these risks. Therefore, the system of distribution of work affected the distribution of accidents among the population.

664 While we were at the shop, we observed that the supervisors' impressions of the people they favoured were correct. The favoured people did, in fact, work harder. But we felt that this was very much the result of a vicious circle. There was a considerable sapping of the morale of the unfavoured people who realised that they were seldom going to be given 'good' jobs and worked according at a more leisurely pace. On the occasions that they did get some 'good' jobs, their attitudes could alter quite dramatically. We thought that a uniform system of distribution of the jobs, especially the 'good' jobs, would have benefited the majority of the staff and given more people an incentive to speed up. This would not necessarily restrict the opportunities of the favoured people, though it would partially reduce the ease with which they could earn bonus doing the 'good' jobs.

M. SIMON

Appendix 31
A brief look at the law

A – THE WORKING ENVIRONMENT (despatch department)

Cleaning
665 Section 1 of the Factories Act 1961 deals with the cleanliness of premises; it requires the daily removal of accumulations of dirt and refuse, and floor cleaning by washing at least once a week or, if it is effective and suitable, by sweeping or other method. At the despatch department, the refuse was swept when necessary from the floors, but usually only when men were available, i.e. if not much work was about. We had a record of which days the refuse was swept, and there was sometimes as much as a fortnight's gap between sweepings. This generally occurred during busy periods at the department. Some refuse was removed unofficially by the men in a temporary fashion, i.e. a group sometimes cleared their area by simply sweeping rubbish on to some other part.

666 Van drivers were supposed to sweep out their own vehicles and this they did but not always as often as was necessary. We recorded one cut caused by glass splinters lying on the floor of a van. Particularly hazardous were the metal bands which often lay loose on the floor. While observing, we occasionally caught our feet in these bands. An accident, which caused a day's absence, was a result of a wooden block being left about with two nails protruding, one of which penetrated the foot of a man who stepped on it.

667 Hygienic conditions were affected by the comparatively rare removal of much of the rubbish during the summer. Rubbish was generally removed from the department once a week, but in that time the smell sometimes became quite bad in hot weather.

Illumination
668 Section 5 requires that where 'persons are working or passing' there should be 'sufficient and suitable lighting'. Normally, during the day, the department was illuminated by daylight coming through the roof lights and doorways, which gave a general illumination on a bright winter's day of around 1700 lux. Artificial lighting was provided by filament bulbs of 300 watts and 400 watts in industrial type reflectors. This gave a general level of illumination which, although mainly in the range 100–140 lux, appeared rather dim when there was little or no daylight. The vans were lit by portable hand-lamps (60 watts) on

trailing cables and these gave a level of illumination from near zero to 100 lux, depending on the position and the shadows cast.

669 In the vans, it was difficult to see parcels and especially see the addresses upon them. It was necessary for the men to carry the hand-lamps. The vans had no built-in source of internal lighting; when there was little or no daylight, the corners were nearly pitch black. The foremen were issued with torches, but surprisingly the men had none. They could, of course, have borrowed a torch from a foreman, but this happened very seldom.

670 Several minor accidents occurred whilst men were working in vans in the early mornings or the evenings of winter, and the lighting factor obviously cannot be ignored, particularly as the main type of accident inside a van was that of colliding with goods already loaded.

Slippery or obstructed floors

671 Section 29(1) states that 'all floors . . . shall, so far as is reasonably practicable, be kept free . . . from any substance likely to cause persons to slip'. The roof at the department leaked badly in wet weather and about two-thirds of the working surface of the floor became damp; puddles formed in some places where the leak was particularly bad. Some of the drainage pipes from the roof had badly fitting joints, and from two of these water gushed out like a waterfall.

672 The floor was sprinkled with sawdust when it became wet to make it less slippery, but even so some men with ordinary footwear tended to slither whilst pushing a heavy barrow. The metal plates, which spanned the gap to a van, and the continuous metal plates which formed part of the floor, were made particularly dangerous by being wet. Many of the plates were not ribbed and rain on the smooth surface made them very slippery, thus increasing the risk of an accident, e.g. one man, helping another who was pushing a loaded barrow, slipped on a metal bridge plate. His right leg went down in the gap and he twisted his knee. This resulted in a lost time accident of $87\frac{1}{2}$ working days. The plates were wet at the time and must be considered an important contributory factor.

673 Section 28(1) also deals with obstruction of floors etc; 'all floors . . . shall, so far as is reasonably practicable, be kept free from obstruction'. There were twelve cranes in the department. They were hand-operated with levers which stood about 3 ft high. The levers were designed to be removed but, through many years of use, they had bent and could not be removed.

674 A serious accident occurred when a man knocked one of the levers in passing, causing the crane to swing, its chain hitting another man on the side of his head. The man sustained bruising, shock, and slight deafness as a result and was absent for most of the year, his medical certificates quoting the latter two symptoms as the cause of his long absence.

675 There is a strong argument for the removal of most of the cranes and the design of new levers which could be fitted and removed for the remainder. This would not be an expensive or difficult task for the maintenance department.

676   Ironically, a Company rule states that 'cranes must be kept locked or otherwise secured when not in use'. This rule was totally ignored by supervisors and, more importantly, by management.

Floor construction and maintenance

677   Section 28(1) also states that all floors etc 'shall be of sound construction and properly maintained'. The floor surface had apparently been a continual source of complaint for many years. It consisted of boards overlaid with asphalt. It had become rutted and worn owing to heavy usage and was sufficiently uneven to affect the transit of a barrow. Many of the ruts had been repaired just before our study commenced but during the course of the year many more ruts appeared, up to 1 in. deep, and these were a hazard to the men. If the wheels of a barrow caught in a rut, the barrow tended to jerk both the load and the barrowman. There was also the possibility of slipping or tripping whilst walking or pushing a barrow. One injury occurred when a man caught his foot in a small rut, strained his ankle and was absent for a few days. One hole (pointed out to me by several people, which showed the extent of the feeling about it) was several inches deep and wide and was obviously a hazard for some days, until it was covered with a metal plate which remained there for two months, when the hole was eventually repaired.

678   The majority of the men complained at one time or another of the condition of the surface, and the management was aware of the problem. Occasional 'make-do' repairs were carried out at week-ends, but this was apparently dependent on whether men were available to do them. These repairs often resulted in a hump where there was previously a hole. We do not think it could be said that the department floor was 'properly maintained' during the year we were there.

M. SIMON

B – MACHINE GUARDS

Section 14

679   The extent to which some details of the safety law, laid out in Sections 13 and 14 of the Factories Act, 1961, were complied with in the assembly and machine shops varied greatly between them and even between sections within them. The risks inherent in the operations differed greatly, and so we must look at these in more detail before we can discuss the extent to which they may be eliminated or reduced.

680   Section 13 is concerned with transmission machinery, Section 14 with other machinery and both are concerned with fencing to prevent operators from coming into contact with parts of the machinery which are dangerous when in motion or in use. The Sections include machinery not driven by mechanical power. A fuller discussion of this can be found in Redgrave's Factories Acts. The duty to fence securely is an absolute one, so that practicability need not be considered; but, in fact, most of the matters described below can be improved by practical devices.

681 In the assembly workshops there were relatively few machines and most of the assembly work was carried out with hand tools and automatic screwdrivers. The two 'sub-assembly' sections did have a few smaller hand presses, and we recorded six accidents where people succumbed to the risk of an unguarded press. In none of the cases was the injury serious, and in at least one instance a guard was fixed to the machine soon after the accident. This is a good example of the effects of local history, on which compliance with Section 14 appears greatly to depend. After the supply of the guard the operators no longer injured themselves in that way. From this it seems as though the people working on and around the machines do not see a risk until someone has succumbed to it (see also Appendix para. 363 *et seq.*).

682 On the assembly lines themselves there were other presses on which accidents occurred. One, incurring a hospital visit, took place when a step ladder, placed near a hand operated press, just touched the handle, causing the sharp tool to fall. A supervisor happened to be working on the machine at the time, and had his finger punctured. In another incident a similar machine did have a guard door, but it was possible to open this before the operation was completed, and the girl operator nipped her thumb between the moving top tool and the fixed part of the machine. In this case the lock of the fencing device was out of adjustment, owing to wear.

683 Other machines used in this workshop which allow operators to come into contact with dangerous parts are the hand operated broaching machines. These have a sharp pointed tool; one hand holds the component in place, the other operates the handle. On three occasions the tool penetrated the operators' fingers instead of the component.

684 We have recorded three accidents where rivets from a foot pedal operated machine entered the operator's finger. Considering the thousands and thousands of rivets which have been driven into holes without incident this would not readily be labelled highly dangerous. However, one accident meant hospital visits and at least one hour off work, illustrating that even this should have been provided with some sort of guard.

685 Similar to this type are two accidents involving an operator who stapled her thumb instead of a strip of ribbon. The stapling machine then became dangerous when used in conjunction with material; this is the subject of some legal controversy.

686 On another type of machine a bezel is 'squeezed' on to a component, which is held in position by a clamp. It is possible for the operator to catch his fingers between the tool and the work, and we recorded three instances of this.

Twice out of the three times the work had stuck and the operator was trying to pull it free. None of the injuries were serious, but the operators may have been lucky, because the machine exerts a great deal of force during the operation.

687   There are risks inherent in operating the machines described above but most of the machinery in this workshop may be said to comply with Sections 13 and 14; had it been otherwise there would have been more accidents that were serious.

688   The machine shop that we studied had nine sections, all of which used different machinery for different jobs, and which varied considerably in the extent to which they complied with Section 14 of the Factories Act. For example, the grinding section has centreless grinders, various types of overhead grinders, and some universal grinders.* Some had the grinding wheels exposed, some were guarded; one had a belt driven head, others were motor driven. There were other types of machines within the section besides grinders; reeling machines, a honing machine, a broach, a fly press, squarers and drills.

689   Most of the grinding wheels were exposed and it was possible to touch the fast-moving wheels. An operator often had to put his fingers very near the wheel and if he miscalculated his timing or placement, he might easily grind part of his fingers off. One of the serious accidents occurred when a pin broke on a jig. The jig and component twisted, dragging a finger under the grinding wheel. As this was clogged with plastic, the operator's finger was rolled rather than cut, saving the top from amputation.

690   On another occasion someone walking past a grinding wheel touched it by mistake. It had been left running even though it was not in use.

691   A less obvious machine risk is caused by the operator's ignorance of a particular mechanism. Two accidents happened on the same machine when the operators switched the wheel into a reverse movement instead of forwards. The machine had been changed some time previously, and neither of the operators had used it since. There was nothing on the machine to indicate what the different switch positions meant.

692   The power presses were guarded by a combination of fixed and interlocked guards. These automatic guards were noticeably better maintained after regular inspection was required by the introduction of the Power Press Regulations, 1965. We did not hear of any accidents in which an *operator* was injured by a moving tool, but two setters were injured by press tools descending on their hands. In one instance, a particular loop-hole had been missed until then; the probable reason is that no one had succumbed to that particular risk before. Soon after the accident the guards were all modified so that not even setters could reach between the tools when the machine was energised.

---

* The application of Section 14 of the Factories Act 1961 to grinding wheels was altered from 2 April 1970 by the Abrasive Wheels Regulations 1970.

693 The safety of the guards themselves is something which safety officers should examine when checking their machines. The gates should be set in such a way that the closing movement is not too fast. The edges which an operator might touch should be smooth, and, in a gate-type guard, covered with strips of rubber. A gate closing quickly and sharply can cause an injury; this in fact happened three times during our study. Sometimes the adjustment of the gate speed is within the scope of the operator, and he adjusts it so that he can work faster and earn a better bonus; the press guard inspector should be able to notice this. Gate speeds should not be alterable except by the use of special tools.

694 In contrast with the well guarded power press section, where few accidents were caused by contact with moving tools, is the drill section, where almost all the drills were exposed, and where we recorded about 55 accidents which arose from apparent breaches of Section 14. These drilling machines are placed close together on work benches. They have from one to four chucks. Seldom were any of these drills guarded in the way the law requires.

695 Jigs are used for some components and for certain operations, e.g. reaming, and the drill is lowered by means of a handle. Although a jig is supposed to reduce risks, we recorded a large number of accidents which occurred when the operators were using the jigs. If an operator is trying to work as fast as possible, the jig is placed very near to the running drill, and while inserting the component into the jig, or moving it, the hand is liable to come into contact with the revolving drill. If a bandage, glove or sleeve is caught in the drill, the situation becomes even more dangerous, and we noted about six of these incidents. Several people cut their fingers during 'offering up'. This practice of bringing work up to a running drill was often used for de-burring. Drills were often used, too, rather than proper roses.

696 In the lathe sections, inserting and removing components while the chuck or collet was running was common. This practice caused six accidents which could be said to result from breaches of Section 14. We found that the operators usually knew that they were not supposed to do this, but continued to do so because it was the only way they could earn a 'decent bonus'. One of the men, whose finger and nail were worn down by the moving collet, regarded the injury lightly, as part of the job. A woman who caught her finger between the collet and the cutter said that she had lost concentration for a second; the result of this split second aberration of timing was at least three quarters of an hour lost time in going to the medical centre for a dressing and re-dressing, as well as the discomfort of the injury.

697 Similar accidents (but not breaches of Section 14) are those in which operators injure themselves on the sharp components which they are handling while the chuck is running. The fact that the machine is in motion increases the severity of the injury. All the injuries of this sort which we saw required treatment at the medical centre.

698 We think that if the statutory requirement to fence dangerous parts of machines could be extended to include the material*, the Factories Act would be far more effective than it is at present. It is illogical to maintain that a machine in motion is dangerous but that the material upon which it is working is 'safe'. In practice, on the factory floor, operators have to guard against moving components just as closely as against machinery in motion. In some of our cases it is difficult to decide where to draw the line, as the agent of injury could have been either the machinery or the material.

699 From this examination of recorded accidents at two workshops we may conclude that compliance with the law is limited by certain factors. First is the degree of enforcement. Secondly, local practice and history in a particular section appears to have a great deal of influence on the extent to which regulations are put into practice. We have mentioned cases where guards were fixed only after an accident had occurred but have also noticed one section in particular where there were several gear-cutting machines which had exposed cutting wheels. There were no guards on these, although they were obviously dangerous. No injury has been recorded on these machines during the two years of our study. A third factor limiting compliance with this Act can be recognised in the system of bonus payment and the necessity to work fast to earn bonus rates. It is for this reason that press gates are sometimes made to work faster than they should do to be safe: that drills are nearer jigs than they should be and that chucks are kept running while components are inserted and removed.

SHELLEY RADICE

---

* It has been put to us that this would sometimes create insuperable difficulty. Trips to the moon were so described at one time. The legislature could allow temporary exemptions, to give the designer time to re-think.

Appendix 32
Notes on the functions of Union safety representatives
PROPOSED IN THE EMPLOYED PERSONS (HEALTH AND SAFETY) BILL
(Bill 104, 1970)

700   The functions of a safety representative are set out in Section 9(1) of the Bill. They are:

(*a*)   *to promote co-operation* between management and workers in achieving and maintaining safe and healthy working conditions in the factory.

(*b*)   *to carry out inspections* in the factory, from time to time, in the interests of the safety and health of the workers.

701   The Bill does not detail further the promotion of co-operation, but it does describe the occasions for the inspections:

(*a*)   A safety representative may, on giving due notice, inspect any or all parts of the factory, but no part may be inspected at an interval shorter than three months.

(*b*)   He may inspect the scene of a notifiable accident or occurrence. (This is not to be counted in calculating the minimum interval of inspections on notice.)

702   These two occasions impose on a safety representative diametrically opposed objectives for his inspection.

703   On the one hand, regular inspection of premises, followed by a reminder to management – informally, by a word in the right ear, or formally, in writing – that some item of prevention work is outstanding, can be a valuable way of promoting co-operation. In effect, the safety representative would reinforce any accident prevention service the management might already have, and would put the workers' point of view. Done properly, this can do nothing but good.

704   On the other hand, inspection after a notifiable accident or occurrence (i.e., a serious accident) will inevitably involve consideration of liability for claims for damages. And, as soon as this enters the picture, management and safety representative range themselves in opposite legal camps. It is true that it would be valuable, especially to a Union, to have the report of an expert examination of the scene by someone trained in the art. But even assuming a safety representative were so trained, his joining a battle about liability would be the finish of the co-operation which he is supposed to engender. Imagine that, on inspection, he finds some fact which plainly indicates negligence on the part of management. Is he to record it one day and seek management's co-operation the next? Imagine that he finds some fact which suggests that the injured worker wilfully disregarded his own safety. Is the representative to record that and live in the same shop as the injured man and his mates? Worse still, supposing the representative records nothing, and the facts emerge at a subsequent hearing of the case by the High Court. How will the safety representative explain his silence?

705 The present legislative provisions for the compensation of persons injured by accident at work create a situation which would be intolerable for a Union safety representative functioning as envisaged in the Bill. Basically, it is these legislative provisions which need modification – the so-called 'compensation lottery' is in urgent need of replacement by a more equitable system. Meanwhile, we think the right of safety representatives to inspect the scene of a notifiable accident or occurrence should be removed from the Bill and replaced by one under which the Union concerned would be able to send in its own external representative to inspect.

P. I. POWELL
(with acknowledgement to Myles White)

Postscript

'No thoughtful man versed in the methods of natural enquiry can fail to be reminded at every moment of the ultimate and universal dependence of every one group of phenomena upon every other.'

– T. C. ALLBUTT (1896) A System of Medicine

Appendix 33
Bibliography

BELBIN, E. (1956). The effects of propaganda on recall, recognition and behaviour: I and II. *British Journal of Psychology*, **47**, 163–174, 259–270.

BRITISH STANDARDS INSTITUTION (1964). Guarding of Machinery. B.S.C.P. 3004:1964.

BUZZARD, R. B. & LIDDELL, F. D. K. (1963). Coalminers' attendance at work. *Medical Research Memorandum 3*. London; National Coal Board Medical Service.

BUZZARD, R. B. & RADFORTH, J. L. (1964). *Statistical records about people at work*. London: NIIP.

CESA-BIANCHI, M. & DI NARO, C. (1964). Recherche sur les attitudes envers les moyens individuels de protection (Research into attitudes towards individual means of protection). *Bulletin du Centre d'Etudes et Recherches Psychotechniques*, **13** (3), 101–117.

CHAPANIS, A. (1967). The Relevance of Laboratory Studies to Practical Situations. *Ergonomics*, **10**, 557–577.

CURSON, C. (1969). Compensation for accidents at work – can we learn from Canada? *Industrial Law Society Bulletin* No. 6, 1–6.

DALTON, K. (1960). Accidents and menstruation. *British Medical Journal*, November, 1425–1426.

DAVIS, D. R. & COILEY, P. A. (1959). Accident-proneness in motor-vehicle drivers. *Ergonomics*, **2**, 239–246.

EUROPEAN COAL AND STEEL COMMUNITY (1967) *Les Facteurs Humains et la Securité dans les Mines et la Siderurgie*. (Etudes de Physiologie et de Psychologie du Travail No. 2) Luxembourg: Communauté Européenne du Charbon et de l'Acier.

FACTORY INSPECTORATE, H. M. (1958–1970) *Safety Health and Welfare*, (*New Series*). London: H.M.S.O.

FACTORY INSPECTORATE, H. M. (1970–   ) *Health and Safety at Work Series*. London: H.M.S.O.

FARMER, E. & CHAMBERS, E. G. (1926). A psychological study of individual differences in accident rates. *Industrial Fatigue Research Board Report* No. 38. London: H.M.S.O.

FAVERGE, J. M. (1970). L'homme agent d'infiabilité et de fiabilité du processus industrial (The operator's reliability and safety in industry). *Ergonomics*, **13**, 301–327.

FIFE, I. & MACHIN, E. A. (1966). *Redgrave's Factories Acts* (21st Edition). London: Butterworth.

FISCHER, H. (1969). Findings of recent studies in psychological accident prevention. *Proceedings of 3rd International Safety Conference*, 7–9 October, 1969.

FROGGATT, P. & SMILEY, J. A. (1964). The concept of accident proneness: a review. *British Journal of Industrial Medicines*, **21**, 1–12.

FUGAL, S. R. (1950). Relationship of safety education to industrial accidents. (Ph.D. thesis, Yale University).

GRISEZ, J. (1957). Note sur les concepts et les methods employés pour l'étude des aspects psychologiques de l'apparition des accidents (Note on concepts and methods used for study of psychological aspects of the occurrence of accidents). *Bulletin du C.E.R.P.*, **6** (3), 257–282.

HADDON, W., SUCHMAN, E. A. & KLEIN, D. (1964) *Accident Research: Methods and Approaches*. New York: Harper and Row.

HAGBERGH, A. (1960) Accidents: the individual, the work and the work situation. *Paradets Med.* (*Stockholm*). No. 23.

LANER, S. & SELL, R. G. (1960). An experiment on the effect of specially designed safety posters. *Occupational Psychology*, **34**, 153–169.

LEES, P. L. (1966). Vulnerability to trauma of women in relation to periodic stress. *In* Medical Commission on Accident Prevention. Second Annual Report 1965–6.

LEPLAT, J. (1961). Psychologie expérimentale et étude des accidents (Experimental pyschology and the study of accidents). *Bulletin du C.E.R.P.*, **10** (4) 473–488.

MCFARLAND, R. A. (1963). Critique of accident research. *Annals of the New York Academy of Science*, **107** (2).

MURRELL, K. F. H. (1965). *Ergonomics*. London: Chapman and Hall.

MURRAY, R. (1969). Sir Alexander Redgrave Memorial Lecture, 1969. (Institution of Industrial Safety Officers).

OSBORNE, E. *et al.* (1922). Two contributions to the study of accident causation A. The influence of temperature and other conditions on the frequency of industrial accidents; by E. E. Osborne and H. M. Vernon, B. On the relation of fatigue and accuracy to speed and duration of work; by B. Muscio. *Industrial Fatigue Research Board Report* No. 19, London: H.M.S.O.

ROBAYE, F. (1963). Quelques propositions pour l'établissement d'un modèle de comportement dans les situations dangereuses (Some propositions for the establishment of a model of behaviour in dangerous situations). *Bulletin du C.E.R.P.*, **12** (4), 331–340.

RUSSELL DAVIS, D. (1966). Railway signals passed at danger: the drivers, circumstances and psychological processes. *Ergonomics*, **9**, 211–222.

SLOCOMBE, C. S. & BRAKEMAN, E. E. (1930). Psychological tests and accident proneness. *British Journal of Psychology*, **21**, 29–38.

SMEED, R. J. (1960). Proneness of drivers to road accidents. *Nature, Lond.*, **186**, 273–275.

VAN ZELST, R. H. (1954). The effect of age and experience upon accident rate. *Journal of Applied Psychology*, **38**, 313–317.

VERNON, H. M. (1936). *Accidents and their Prevention*. London: Cambridge University Press.

VOCE, J. T. (1969). *The Injured Workman*. Esher: G. and M.W.U.

WALKER, C. R. & GUEST, R. H. (1952). *The Man on the Assembly Line.* Cambridge, Mass.: Harvard University Press.

WELFORD, A. T. (1958). *Ageing and Human Skill.* London: Oxford University Press for the Nuffield Foundation.

WINSEMIUS, W. (1965). Some ergonomic aspects of safety. *Ergonomics,* **8,** 151–162.

WINSEMIUS, W. (1969), Some observations on task-structures and disturbances in relation to safety. *Proceedings of a Symposium on Ergonomics in Machine Design, jointly organised by the Czechoslovak Medical Society, J. E. Purkyne and ILO. Prague, 2–7 October 1967.* Geneva: ILO .

N.B. – There are some references to publications about NOISE in the appendix on it (para. 566), and to REPETITIVE MANUAL WORK IN RELATION TO ACCIDENTS in Paul Branton's appendix (para. 547).

A. R. HALE
MARY HALE